ROUSSEAU'S
THE SOCIAL CONTRACT

CONTINUUM *READER'S GUIDES*

Continuum's *Reader's Guides* are clear, concise and accessible introductions to classic works of philosophy. Each book explores the major themes, historical and philosophical context and key passages of a major philosophical text, guiding the reader toward a thorough understanding of often demanding material. Ideal for undergraduate students, the guides provide an essential resource for anyone who needs to get to grips with a philosophical text.

READER'S GUIDES AVAILABLE FROM CONTINUUM:

ROUSSEAU'S
THE SOCIAL CONTRACT

A READER'S GUIDE

CHRISTOPHER D. WRAIGHT

continuum

Continuum International Publishing Group
The Tower Building   80 Maiden Lane
11 York Road   Suite 704
London SE1 7NX   New York NY 10038

British Library Cataloguing-in-Publication Data
A catalogue record for this book is available from the British Library.

ISBN-10: HB: 0-8264-9859-0
PB: 0-8264-9860-4
ISBN-13: HB: 978-0-8264-9859-5
PB: 978-0-8264-9860-1

Library of Congress Cataloguing-in-Publication Data
Wraight, Christopher D.
Rousseau's the social contract : a reader's guide / Christopher D.Wraight.
p. cm.
ISBN 978-0-8264-9859-5 – ISBN 978-0-8264-9860-1
1. Rousseau, Jean-Jacques, 1712-1778. Du contrat social. I. Title.

JC179.R88W73 2008
320.1'1–dc22

2008014322

Typeset by Newgen Imaging Systems Pvt Ltd, Chennai, India
Printed and bound in Great Britain by MPG Books Ltd,
Bodmin, Cornwall

CONTENTS

PREFACE

Rousseau's *The Social Contract* is one of the most important and influential works of political philosophy ever written. Since its publication in 1762, it has enthused, enraged, provoked, inspired and frustrated its readers in equal measure. Though relatively short and attractively written, it is not an easy book to come to grips with. Despite Rousseau's rhetorical skills and a gift for the memorable phrase, the ideas he treats are difficult and profound. His main issue is the proper place of the individual within society, and particularly how political institutions may best be organized so that the citizens of the state can flourish and prosper. As we shall see, in addressing this question he makes use of a subtle and original thesis of human nature and psychology, without which the political arguments that follow are hard to understand. Rousseau's aims are ambitious: he wishes to demonstrate how people might find a way of living which respects and enhances their natural capacity for moral fulfilment. Though the answers he arrives at have by no means convinced all his readers, the text of *The Social Contract* is replete with insight into the human condition and the forces which govern it, and is as instructive as it is challenging.

It is often thought that Rousseau's political ideas are too inconsistent to be wholly convincing, and that though *The Social Contract* may contain some insights of genius, it does not possess sufficient rigour to be taken seriously as a coherent whole. Certainly, it seems to me that there are several instances where Rousseau appears to change the tenor of his views on key issues at different points in the text (such as the likely success of the sovereign's self-regulation). Moreover, the brief or scattered descriptions of such important concepts as the general will and the role of the lawgiver make it difficult to derive a wholly convincing picture of either. However, I hope that this guide will illustrate the extent to which Rousseau's psychological and political ideas do follow from one another. In common with most commentators on Rousseau, I have taken as my starting point the ideas on human nature articulated in two important prior works, the *Discourse on the Sciences and Arts* and the *Discourse on the Origin of Inequality*. With something of an understanding of the argument of these essays, the moves made in *The Social Contract* make more sense.

In considering the text itself, I have only departed from the order of chapters once, where it seemed to me that the discussion of the general will in the first two sections of Book IV properly belonged together with its initial presentation in Book II. Otherwise, each section of this guide corresponds to a chapter or consecutive group of chapters in the original. At the end of the discussion of each of Rousseau's four books, there is a short summary and a set of study questions. Quotes from *The Social Contract* are indicated in parentheses after the relevant extract in the form (*SC*, b, c), where 'b' is the book and 'c' is the chapter. Other references are cited in the notes at the end of the book. The text used throughout is Maurice Cranston's translation, though there are a number of other editions available in English. Details of these and other works quoted in this book are to be found in the final chapter on further reading.

In preparing this guide I have used a number of works of secondary literature. The most important have been Nicholas Dent's *A Rousseau Dictionary* and *Rousseau: An Introduction to his Psychological, Social and Political Theory*; Robert Wokler's *Rousseau* for the Past Masters series; and Christopher Bertram's *Rousseau and the Social Contract*. Each has been invaluable in helping to interpret Rousseau's sometimes perplexing arguments, and I am indebted to all. Any errors or misinterpretations remaining are, of course, my sole responsibility.

I have been lucky enough to receive the support of friends and family during the writing of this book, for which I am very grateful. I am especially appreciative of the contributions made by Christopher Warne and Dr Iain Law, who were generous enough to comment on drafts of the work. I am also in debt to Tom Crick and Sarah Douglas at Continuum for their patience and guidance during the preparation of the manuscript.

CHAPTER 1

CONTEXT

POLITICAL AND INTELLECTUAL ENVIRONMENT

Jean-Jacques Rousseau lived through a period of profound social and political change in Europe. He was born in 1712 during the final years of Louis XIV, who was the model of an absolute, autocratic monarch. Just over ten years after his death in 1778, the Bastille was stormed by revolutionaries and the days of the French monarchy were drawing to a close. During his lifetime, the foundations of the industrial revolution were laid, the steam engine was invented and European explorers were pushing the boundaries of colonization and commerce further into Asia, North America and the Pacific. In the arts, the baroque magnificence of Bach and Rameau was gradually replaced by the cool brilliance of Mozart and Haydn, while a radical new form of literature, the novel, was establishing itself through the works of Swift, Fielding and Voltaire. Philosophers and thinkers such as David Hume, Adam Smith, John Locke, Benjamin Franklin and Immanuel Kant were making seminal contributions to questions of metaphysics, religion, economics, morality and political theory.

One of the remarkable features of Rousseau's career is that he con-tributed to so many of these various fields of activity. In his own lifetime, he was as famous (or infamous) as a novelist, composer and playwright as he was a political thinker. Through his ideas of human nature and the legitimate basis of society, the subjects of *The Social Contract*, are now his most widely celebrated achievements; he also made notable contributions to the development of literature, music and educational practice. Rather than simply reflecting the tastes and preoccupations of his age, he helped to challenge and shape them. Despite being only intermittently accepted into the mainstream of intellectual society, and frequently capable of marginalizing himself through a mix of radicalism and paranoia, after his death his stock rose considerably. He is now seen as one of the principal architects of the Age of Enlightenment in Europe and a political philosopher of signal importance.

In assessing this legacy, it is helpful to have a very brief overview of some aspects of the environment in which he was writing. The first of these was the growing prestige and success of the natural sciences. Freed from the destructive religious conflict and lingering feudalism of the previous century, educated men (and it was mostly men) in a comparatively wealthy and peaceful age were able to bend their efforts towards the creation and refinement of new inventions in a whole range of disciplines. In the great centres of population such as London and Paris, the exchange of ideas had never been greater. Theoretical advances in physics, chemistry and mathematics achieved in earlier years were used to create practical solutions to problems of agricultural production, transport, architecture and medicine. It seemed to many that the application of critical, enquiring, rational thought was the solution to almost any kind of problem. In great contrast to our own doubting and pessimistic age, the intelligentsia of Rousseau's time were mostly struck by how well they were doing, and by the possibility of further improvement. Exploration of the less-developed wider world outside Europe would have generally reinforced their impression of living in a uniquely technologically advanced, progressive and powerful society.

Alongside scientific progress, great changes in social and moral thinking were also occurring. The enquiring mentality which produced the impressive technologies of the age was also apt to question long-established political and religious conventions. In particular, the grip of the established churches over the dissemination and inculcation of moral teaching was eroded by a small but influential number of critical commentators, increasingly unafraid of either spiritual or temporal punishment. In Paris, a loose collection of intellectuals known as the *philosophes* epitomized this spirit of irreverent enquiry. One of the foremost members of the movement, Denis Diderot, was the driving force behind the great manifesto of the Enlightenment, the *Encyclopaedia*. Aside from his project's ambitious objective of cataloguing the entire state of contemporary human knowledge, Diderot and his fellow contributors used their varied collection of articles to present the case for religious tolerance. The key tenets of the Church were to be subject to the same process of rational dissection and examination as every other set of beliefs. Though there was considerable resistance to many of these ideas, and Diderot himself faced chronic harassment and persecution from the ecclesiastical authorities in France, the fact that such a compendium could be published at all was indicative of how far the power of the Church to stifle criticism had waned since the era of the religious wars.

Of course, it was a matter of considerable debate, as it has been ever since, whether or not this freedom to criticize was a good thing. Europe's political authorities, most of whom derived at least part of their authority from association with religious institutions, were divided in their response to the restless intellectual curiosity of the *philosophes* and their ilk. Sympathetic rulers, such as Frederick II of Prussia, enacted reforms enabling greater freedom of thought and expression; others, like Louis XV of France, were more cautious in tolerating dissent. And although there were a number of itinerant writers like Diderot agitating for more social and intellectual freedoms, there was also a powerful body of thought arguing for authoritarian, conservative rule. The political theorist Hugo Grotius, who was considered an authority on the rights of princes and is often quoted by Rousseau, argued that citizens of a state gave up their own rights to a ruler in exchange for the protection of their lives and property, and that there was no justification in rising up against repressive or tyrannical regimes.[1]

So Rousseau's age was one of intellectual disturbance, with powerful forces for change (technology, secularism, political reform) ranged against equally powerful forces of tradition and stability (the Church, monarchical government). In many respects, it was the period when the foundations of a recognizably modern Europe were beginning to be laid. Though many of the reformists' ideas were later to play a dominant role in creating the social institutions we see around us today, it would have been by no means obvious at the time that their project was anything other than a passing phase. As we shall see, Rousseau's work, not least *The Social Contract*, played a significant part in this clash of ideas.

LIFE AND WRITINGS

As a man, Rousseau was by any standards an extraordinary character. Far from the stereotype of a cloistered, mild-mannered academic, he travelled widely during his eventful life, driven from place to place by a passionate, inquiring mind (or, at times, the displeasure of those whom he had offended). His intense, sometimes baffling preoccupations and opinions caught the imagination of many of his contemporaries, while being equally capable of rousing violent opposition. Rousseau was a profoundly divisive figure, both for the revolutionary ideas expressed in his various writings, and for the erratic conduct of his personal affairs and relations. Indeed, the relationship between his constantly evolving thought and his turbulent private life is always close, making it more than usually useful to have at least a cursory understanding of the latter before attempting to engage with the former.

The richest source of information on Rousseau's life is his remarkably frank autobiography, *The Confessions*, a huge and at times thoroughly entertaining account of his personal and intellectual development. There are also a number of works written at the end of his life, some shrill and self-justificatory, others reflective and insightful. Together, they reveal a man endlessly preoccupied with the thorniest questions of human relations: What is the fundamental nature of people? How best may their social affairs be organized? What prevents them from fulfilling their proper potential? While his autobiographical writings are often harsh on the failings of others to conform to his exacting answers to those questions, he is no less judgemental about his own shortcomings. At his worst, Rousseau can come across as paranoid and self-obsessed; at his best, he is capable of commenting with a rare clarity and perceptiveness on human frailty and its capacity for improvement. These are the themes which animate his most important books, not least *The Social Contract*, written fairly late in his life in 1762, and which is principally responsible for his reputation as a political philosopher.

An interest in political questions seems to have been with him from a very early age. Rousseau was born in Geneva in 1712, then an independent city state run along republican lines originally set down by the Protestant theologian John Calvin. In contrast to the hereditary monarchies which then ruled over most of Europe, Geneva was governed by a group of legislative councils drawn from the citizens of the city. Although the system was less genuinely representative than perhaps originally intended (eligible 'citizens' actually made up a relatively small proportion of the population), many Genevois were both acutely conscious and proud of their republic's distinctive constitution. Among them was Rousseau's father, Isaac, who was responsible for Jean-Jacques' initial education. In *The Confessions*, the young Rousseau recalls the discussions he had with his father, based on readings of Plutarch and other classical authors, and attributes his lifelong political sympathies and interests to them:

> It was this enthralling reading, and the discussions it gave rise to between my father and myself, that created in me that proud and intractable spirit, that impatience with the yoke of servitude, which has afflicted me throughout my life [. . .]. Continuously preoccupied with Rome and Athens, living as one might say with their great men, myself born the citizen of a republic and the son of a father whose patriotism was his strongest passion, I took fire by his example and pictured myself as a Greek or Roman.[2]

Despite these fond early memories, Rousseau's childhood was not destined to be stable. His mother had died shortly after bearing him, and in her absence the fortunes of the family declined. When Rousseau was ten, his father fled Geneva following a dispute, leaving him in the care of an uncle. Thenceforth, his life would never again be truly settled. In 1728, after a somewhat piecemeal continuance of his education and a difficult period of apprenticeship, the occasion of being locked outside the gates of the city one evening prompted him to take the bold step of running away and seeking his fortunes elsewhere. After some fairly aimless wandering, he ended up being taken in by the Baronne de Warens, François-Louise de la Tour, with whom he was to have intimate relations on and off for the next twelve years. She introduced him to Catholicism, to which he converted, and also formal musical training. He gradually assumed more responsibility within her idiosyncratic household, and when he was twenty-one became her sexual partner, though on a rather unequal basis. Under her tutelage, Rousseau resumed the reading and study he so much enjoyed, and later looked back on his years at her house in Chambéry with considerable nostalgia. When relations eventually cooled in 1740 and he was forced to move on once more, it was the cause of a period of illness, depression and uncertainty.

The trigger for an upturn in his fortunes was his move to Paris in 1742 with the intention of making his name as a composer and playwright. Success was initially elusive, but the gradual accumulation of contacts and a persistence in the face of adversity resulted in a steadily increasing profile in the city. After ten years of struggle, a performance of his opera, *Le Devin du Village* was given before the King at Fontainebleau, and was an enormous success. It was the pinnacle of his career as a composer. Had he wished it, he could perhaps have worked further on his operatic plans, but by then he was already preoccupied with a campaign against him, real or imagined, among many of the dominant figures in Parisian musical life. In any case, opera was far from the only interest he had cultivated in Paris. During the long period of relative difficulty in establishing himself as a composer and playwright, he had become friendly with several leading members of the Paris intelligentsia. Most important among these was Diderot, who was then engaged on the production of the *Encyclopaedia*. Rousseau was contracted to write articles on music for the project, the contents of which contributed to the further deterioration of his already poisonous relationship with Jean-Philippe Rameau, then the leading composer in France. Yet his writing was destined to move beyond articles on musical theory, and turn back to the topics which had fascinated him as a child.

In his own account, the epiphany came on the road to Vincennes, where he was due to visit Diderot. While reading a newspaper, he chanced across an advertisement for an essay competition run by the Dijon Academy with the subject 'Has the progress of sciences and arts done more to corrupt morals or improve them?' Rousseau records that 'the moment I read this, I beheld another Universe and became another man.'[3] Certainly, from the point at which he decided to enter the competition, ideas were stirred up which proved difficult to dislodge, and were to dominate the literary output of his later life. In 1750, his entry, later published as the *Discourse on the Sciences and Arts*, won the prize. This was followed by a second essay, *Discourse on the Origin of Inequality*, which also achieved success. Although at the time of their publication Rousseau was still best known as a composer, his forays into the world of social criticism were to prove in the long run a greater source of fame (or infamy, depending on the contemporary reader's point of view). We will look at some of the themes of these early works in due course, but the most important feature to note here was the distinct lack of enthusiasm in them for the much-lauded technological and social achievements of the age. In the first *Discourse,* he answers the Academy's question firmly in the negative, and argues that progress in the arts and sciences has a deleterious effect on moral character. Swimming thus heavily against the prevailing tide, it is perhaps no surprise that his early essays became the source of some fame and much controversy.

During this period of intellectual upheaval, Rousseau's personal life continued its rather chaotic course. He settled down to something approaching family life with a barely literate laundry maid named Thérèse Levasseur. She was to stick by him for the rest of his life despite his seemingly casual disregard for her interests: though he finally married her in 1768, there is little to suggest he felt much more than a passing affection for her, and he certainly felt free to indulge in hopeless romances with socially more accomplished women such as Sophie d'Houdetot while he and Thérèse were ostensibly living as man and wife. Thérèse was to bear him five children, all of whom were given away to the foundling hospital. The motivation for this apparently callous behaviour is hard to fathom, and was a source of much criticism from Rousseau's enemies in the years to come. Certainly, he comes out of his relations with Thérèse looking shabby at the least; though she was certainly his intellectual inferior, she emerges from *The Confessions* as a figure of near saintly forbearance.

Bolstered by the success of the two *Discourses* and the support of members of the intelligentsia in Paris, between 1760 and 1762 Rousseau produced his most influential works. Among them was *Julie, or the New Héloïse*, an epistolary novel which achieved great acclaim and ran into many editions. During the same period, he also produced much writing on contemporary politics and social organization. Several projects from this time were never completed, but he did finish his two great books on the individual and society: *Émile, or on Education*, and *The Social Contract*. Unfortunately for him, the ideas contained in both proved too controversial for his audience, especially the sections on organized religion. Outrage at the sentiments expressed in *Émile* in particular led to official condemnation of the books, and Rousseau's flight from France, with Thérèse, to Switzerland. He stayed there for some time under the protection of Frederick II of Prussia, and was briefly able to develop some of his political ideas further, but the enmity he had generated among even some of his erstwhile supporters in France pursued him, and his house was stoned. A bizarre period followed in which Rousseau became increasingly embittered and paranoid about the origins of his persecution. He spent some time in England as the guest of the great Scottish philosopher David Hume, but their relationship broke down in mutual acrimony. From this time onwards, his mental state, never a model of perfect stability, was subject to a marked deterioration.

After being given permission by the authorities, Rousseau returned to France in 1767, where he was to remain for the rest of his life. He continued to write on politics and music, as well as producing a number of autobiographical works. His stock as a composer was still relatively high, as was his reputation with the more radical elements of the Parisian intellectual scene. His position was never entirely secure, however: alongside those who had hated him from the start, such as Rameau and fellow *philosophe* Voltaire, Rousseau had long since alienated some of his closest allies, among them Diderot. One of his final books, the *Reveries of a Solitary Walker*, begins 'So now I am all alone in the world, with no brother, neighbour or friend, nor any company left but my own.'[4] His mental state continued to veer erratically, and he saw plots against him in every quarter. In a typically eccentric final twist, it took a collision with a large dog in which he was badly injured to restore some sense of calm to his disordered mind. The final few years of his life were spent in relative serenity, and he died in 1778 in Ermenonville, near Paris. Though much discouraged by what he saw as the series of conspiracies and injustices which had brought him low, he had retained a good deal of his celebrity cachet throughout his turbulent later life. His works were read as avidly after his death as they had been in life, and posthumously his reputation rose considerably. In 1794, his remains were interred in the Panthéon, the resting place of many of the greatest thinkers, artists and statesmen of France. Though his personal foibles and vices are still open to view through the candid account of *The Confessions*, they have long since ceased to be of as much interest as his philosophical and political legacy, which is the reason he continues to be studied and argued over in the modern age.

CHAPTER 2

OVERVIEW OF THEMES

Like many creative and individual thinkers, Rousseau's psychology was complex and often difficult. As we have seen, he was seldom able to conduct his own affairs for long with any degree of tranquillity. He leapt at enthusiasms with a fervour which only rarely lasted long enough for him to gain true proficiency. While he was quick to form fast friendships with the many individuals he came across during his travels, he was equally adept at turning them into bitter enemies. In many ways, he was a fundamentally contradictory character. He ardently wished for success and to be recognized as a man of substance, but despised glory-seeking and was capable of utterly idolizing simple-minded, benign characters like Mme de Warens. He pursued the bright lights of Paris, and under their illumination was inspired to write his most enduring works, yet forever yearned for the simplicity of the countryside where he would be free to walk in solitude with his notebook and pencil. Essentially, he was a man ill at ease with the world, especially the salons of the intellectual classes which he patronized for many years, tongue-tied and ever ready to commit some fresh indiscretion or faux pas.

With such an uncomfortable relationship with his environment, it is perhaps not surprising that his mature writing is permeated with a deep mistrust of the civilized, urbane form of society exemplified by the Paris of the eighteenth century. Especially in the mostly unhappy final half of his life, Rousseau was liable to compare its vices with an idealized rustic Swiss bliss, part-imagined from his own childhood. Against the fast-talking *philosophes*, who thrived on the cut and thrust of intellectual debate and its accompanying social delights, Rousseau was to develop a philosophy repudiating much of what they stood for. In an age when the power of reason seemed to have achieved so much and promised even more, Rousseau remained sceptical: though scientific and social progress might seem to be the instrument by which great things were achieved, it was also the cause of deep psychological misery and moral malaise. Only by organizing social affairs in such a way as to counteract the worst follies of civilization could the essentially decent nature of men and women be properly realized.[1]

This is one of the central themes of much of his writing, including *The Social Contract*, and the view for which Rousseau is probably most famous. It is frequently characterized as the idea of the 'noble savage': the notion that, free of the corruption of civilization, people are able to live lives of natural honesty, goodness and psychological calm. In all of Rousseau's political writings, the theme of the corrupting influence of poorly constructed societies versus a human natural potential for fulfilment and prosperity is never far from the surface. Naturally enough, thoughts on how bad societies are constructed leads to thoughts on what might be done to repair the damage, and restore something of the virtue of a pre-civilized state. Rousseau's later works are an expression of these ideas for an alternative kind of community, one in which people are not corrupted by the institutions which dominate the development of their moral characters. As he writes in *The Confessions*, referring to the origins of *The Social Contract*,

> I had seen that everything is rooted in politics and that, whatever might be attempted, no people would ever be other than the nature of their government made them. So the great question of the best possible government seemed to me to reduce itself to this: 'What is the nature of the government best fitted to create the most virtuous, the most enlightened, the wisest, and, in fact, the best people, taking the word "best" in its highest sense?'[2]

In the following chapters, we will look at Rousseau's vision for this 'best possible government' in some detail. But for now we should spend some time to examine what he means by 'the best people, taking the word "best" in its highest sense'. Without some understanding of what Rousseau takes the goal of human development to be, or indeed what kinds of human qualities are admirable and worthy of promotion, we will be unable properly to assess his ideas on political and social organization, nor to see why he makes the moves he does in the arguments to come. The remainder of this chapter is an outline of some of these basic concepts, before we consider the text itself later on.

HUMAN NATURE

It is common in political philosophy, when attempting to start from first principles, to appeal to the set of conditions obtaining in a so-called 'state of nature'. Rousseau's predecessors, Thomas Hobbes and John Locke, had made much of this device. As Locke puts it,

> To understand political power right, and derive it from its original, we must consider what state men are naturally in, and that is, a state of perfect freedom to order their actions, and dispose of their possessions, and persons as they think fit, within the bounds of the law of nature.[3]

The idea behind this is to try and get at the way things were, or may have been, prior to the rise of an 'unnatural' civilization. For some philosophers, the state of nature may be treated as a matter of historical fact – a real phase of historical social development which can be theorized about; for others, it may merely be a useful device to introduce some ideas about the relationship between people as they are and people as they might be. In both cases, one intention behind introducing the idea of a state of nature is to try and construct a picture of what people are like *in themselves*; that is, before the meddlesome effects of formal education, law and convention have altered things irretrievably.

Rousseau is no exception to this. Indeed, he felt that others who had made recourse to such a device had not gone far enough: in imagining a state of nature, they had merely come up with a more basic version of the society they already inhabited.[4] His ambitions were more radical: he thought it was possible to have a clear sense of what people were like 'in themselves', and to trace how modern forms of civilization had distorted this original character. These days, even with much greater knowledge of the far past than Rousseau possessed, we might be quite cautious about speculating on the moral character and intentions of those living in pre-civilized times. It is very difficult to imagine what the inner lives of such people could have been like, especially given the paucity of written evidence. Rousseau, however, had no such worries. In his *Discourse on the Origin of Inequality*, he makes two confident claims about the benign character of men and women before they were messed-up by modern society.[5]

The first of these is that, originally, human beings were independent of one another. Unlike the inhabitants of complex modern societies, who are all dependent on an extensive web of others to provide their needs, in a simpler past people were more readily able to meet their requirements without the help of others. Technology plays a large part in this. A professional worker in Rousseau's time (and, for that matter, our own) was incapable of leading a simple, self-sufficient life. They were dependent on an array of others to enable them to work: manufacturers, maintainers and suppliers. And once they had spent time employed using such technology, they depended on an extensive system of banking and finance to enable themselves to convert their labour into money. And then specialists were required to produce the goods which they needed to buy in order to live: food, drink, shelter, heat, etc. They were dependent on all of these people to live their life, and vice versa. According to Rousseau, in the distant past this was very different. People living in a more subsistence-based environment, producing their basic needs themselves, were not beholden to the vast interconnected matrix of give and take which characterizes his and our world. Instead, they were able to provide for themselves in isolation, and had little reason to interact with others unless they wished it. He paints an intriguing picture of

> man in a state of nature, wandering up and down the forests, without industry, without speech, and without home, an equal stranger to war and to all ties, neither standing in need of his fellow-creatures nor having any desire to hurt them [. . .]; let us conclude that, being self-sufficient and subject to so few passions, he could have no feelings or knowledge but such as befitted his situation, [. . .] and that his understanding made no greater progress than his vanity.[6]

A consequence of this distant, happy state of affairs is that people were freer to indulge their natural capacity for compassion. Compassion is a fundamental concept in Rousseau's vision of human nature. Indeed, he thought it one of the most important ingredients for harmonious relations between people and for a successful social order. In the state of nature, where interactions are voluntary and non-coercive, human beings are readier to exercise their natural empathy for one another. One reason for this is that everyone is on the same level, each working independently and peaceably on their own projects, and no oppressive hierarchies exist to generate selfish concern for one's station and rights. Another is that in an environment free of artificial, forced relationships, resentment and envy have yet to cloud the spontaneous capacity of human beings to feel for and with one another. According to Rousseau, all of us by default have a deep-seated and primordial repugnance at another sentient being suffering distress: in the absence of other interfering factors, we will be motivated to help such a person. This is one of the defining characteristics of what it is to be human. In the state of nature, there is nothing to subvert this fundamental drive. As a result, the mutual exercise of compassion produces a harmonious environment in which self-sufficient individuals are only drawn to interact with each other on the basis of a natural desire to avoid suffering:

> It is this compassion that hurries us without reflection to the relief of those who are in distress: it is this which in a state of nature supplies the place of laws, morals, and virtues, with the advantage that none are tempted to disobey its gentle voice.[7]

So two principal features of humanity's natural state, for Rousseau, are freedom from dependence, and the prominent exercise of compassion. These are important claims, and form the starting point of Rousseau's social analysis. But how convincing are they? Is it really likely that humans of the past were independent of each other to the extent suggested by Rousseau? And is the drive for compassion truly of an especially privileged nature compared with other human motivations, such as competition or hostility?

To some extent, in assessing these claims we are as blind as Rousseau. We certainly can't go back to a putative state of nature in order to verify what he says it was like. Nonetheless, it is certainly possible to doubt his assumptions. While it is probable that some pre-civilized communities were less complex and interdependent than ours or Rousseau's, it seems unlikely that there has ever been a state of affairs where people were not forced into some relationships of dependence upon one another. The production of food, shelter and clothing are all activities where it is hard to see how some degree of cooperation, barter or coercion aren't likely, even essential. The idea that there was ever a historical period in which environmental or psychological pressures didn't force people to band together in hierarchies, or raid one another's living spaces, or enter some kind of formal trading arrangement, seems fanciful. Similarly, while few would deny that compassion is an important facet of our makeup as human beings, it is far from obvious that it would assume a uniquely prominent position in the absence of familiar social institutions. As we shall see, Rousseau himself contrasts this drive with the potentially conflicting instinct for self-preservation. In very primitive contemporary societies, in which little technology or complex social structure exists, people display the full range of drives and motivations so familiar to us degenerate denizens of the developed world. Similarly, in the social groupings of animals most closely related to us, like the great apes, there is as much oppression, violence and envy as there is in our own. All of this casts doubt on the utopian vision conjured up in Rousseau's state of nature.[8]

Nonetheless, while we may reasonably doubt the historical veracity of Rousseau's claims, there is no need yet to reject his analysis of our social ills entirely. Moving into the present, it may be true that excessive social interdependence, formalized in relationships of coercion and constraint, is a significant drain on our otherwise natural capacity for happiness and compassion. And in fact Rousseau goes into some detail to show how this happens using a set of concepts which deserve our attention.

PSYCHOLOGY AND SOCIETY

In the *Discourse on the Origin of Inequality*, Rousseau writes that,

> *amour de soi-même* is a natural feeling which leads every animal to look to its own preservation, and which, guided in man by reason and modified by compassion, creates humanity and virtue.[9]

The phrase '*amour de soi-même*', or *amour de soi*, may be translated 'love of oneself', or 'self-love'. For Rousseau, this is the most natural inclination existing in people, and one of the important aspects of his psychology. Self-love may seem a rather odd basis of human behaviour, given what has been said earlier about the essentially benign and compassionate state of pre-civilized society. However, in Rousseau's use, it does not mean, as it often does in English, an excessive self-regard or vanity. For that reason, English-speaking commentators on Rousseau often leave the phrase untranslated. Instead, what Rousseau means is that a healthy desire for the preservation of our self is the basis for all our other drives. In the absence of other corrupting inclinations, this is an entirely healthy and proper thing. After all, if we were not disposed to safeguard our well-being to some degree, life would be a contradictory and capricious thing. This, at its simplest level, is all that *amour de soi* means: the natural instinct to look after ourselves and seek a prosperous, secure path through life.

It is a drive which other living things share, of course. Animals, through instinct, seek the same thing. There is not much difference, for Rousseau, between the animal instinct for self-preservation and the human feeling of *amour de soi*, at least in the beginning. However, human beings have a much greater sense of rationality, as well as an ability to learn and plan into the future. So whereas the instinct for self-preservation in an animal is limited to an immediate drive to avoid harm and seek things known to be beneficial, in people it can be transformed into a more sophisticated motivation. On reflection, it may appear to us that certain long-term goals are more conducive to happiness and fulfilment than short-term satisfaction of the appetites. In such a case, *amour de soi* may become a motivation to work towards more lofty ambitions, to shape a form of life best suited to the high value we place on our existence. The belief that our lives are worth preserving and looking after soon extends into the idea that our lives are intrinsically significant, and that things ought to be organized in order to maximize our potential for growth and development. In the state of nature, where human associations are imagined as being loose and non-coercive, *amour de soi* is not in competition with our tendency for compassion: with our lively imaginations, we are quite capable of recognizing the value of other people's lives as well as our own, and may readily assist others in the fulfilment of their goals.

However, the natural goodness of *amour de soi* is highly susceptible to corruption. Whatever we think of the historical likelihood of Rousseau's state of nature, we can be certain that such a utopia doesn't exist now, and it is easy to see how the desire to preserve one's own livelihood and ambitions could come into conflict with those of others. Indeed, Rousseau believes that under the pressure of a complex society, in which we are increasingly bound by networks of dependence on one another, the benign *amour de soi* soon becomes the (potentially) malign *amour-propre*. This, confusingly enough, may also be translated as 'self-love', but the sense here is slightly closer to what we would normally understand by the English phrase. In the *Discourse on the Origin of Inequality*, Rousseau writes,

> *amour-propre* is only a relative sentiment, factitious, and born in society, which inclines every individual to set greater store by himself than by anyone else, inspires men with all the evils they do one another, and is the genuine source of honour.[10]

Amour-propre is the development of the healthy drive towards self-preservation into a more troublesome desire to ensure that one's existence is acknowledged by others. It is usually characterized as a negative drive, but there is some uncertainty over Rousseau's precise intentions for this notion. Some commentators have argued that the basic motivations behind *amour-propre* are harmless and perfectly appropriate. It is quite proper to want to be recognized as a valuable member of society, and for one's dignity and honour to be respected. However, it is very easy for this drive to degrade, especially if we come to see our significance as being challenged by others. If we are insecure in our own estimation and believe that our position in society is being undervalued, then the desire for recognition can turn into an 'inflamed' or malign wish to impose our sense of self-importance on others. The admirable self-worth which we are led towards by our feelings of *amour de soi* is replaced by an inflated sense of our own significance, which leads to strife and competition. In the absence of a social order based on hierarchy and inequality, there may be insufficient catalyst to transform our worthy natural urges into the base metal of malign *amour-propre*. However, when we come into regular association with one another, at least in poorly constituted societies, the competition for resources and prestige accelerates and reinforces an innate tendency to lapse into self-importance and one-upmanship.[11]

When Rousseau criticizes the mores of his time, and is pessimistic about the beneficial effects of the arts and sciences, it is the descent into malign *amour-propre* which he worries about. According to his analysis, his own civilized age (and, we may imagine, ours too) is distorted by an overweening desire by all to establish themselves at the expense of everyone else. Though this constant tension may be creative, in the sense that enormous technological or artistic change may occur, it is nonetheless profoundly damaging in at least two senses. First, political inequalities and injustices develop and become entrenched, as the powerful usurp privileges and advantages from the weak. Second, the psychological health of all of us is diminished, as we move further and further away from the simple aspirations of our 'natural', pre-civilized condition. In such a social order, the possibility of true happiness and fulfilment is always far away: individuals are compelled to strive for superficial tokens of achievement, and are set against each other. The losers in such a struggle are made unhappy by the denial of status and the frustration of their *amour-propre*. Even those who succeed in achieving their goals are not truly happy, since they have only satisfied a perverse and empty objective, rather than the satisfying and natural *amour de soi*.

It is not entirely clear what Rousseau thought the best solution to this sorry state of affairs might be. According to some commentators, he believed that only a return to something like a pre-civilized state could possibly enable human beings to realize their true potential for morality and happiness.[12] Rousseau cannot have consistently intended this as a realistic proposition: the existence of the worked-out political system expounded in *The Social Contract* is a reason for thinking that he believed human beings *could* live harmonious and productive lives even within a complex and 'civilised' social order, bound by laws and governed by institutions. Against this, however, is a deep and frequently recurring pessimism about the capacity of people to retain the best facets of their character, no matter how good the social institutions which govern them are – we will see this later on in our discussion of Rousseau's views on government. But though he is often gloomy about the effects of political systems on the natural human capacity for goodness, it seems unlikely that he consistently thought all forms of society were doomed to fail, since he goes to great lengths to develop his own, positive theories of political organization.

So, to sum up the ideas which drive the development of *The Social Contract*, we might bring these thoughts together as follows. People are endowed with the capacity for goodness and compassion. It is possible to imagine a pre-social state of affairs in which these capacities are allowed to flourish to their full potential. Such a state may have even existed. In any case, there is also a form of social interaction, characterized by unequal relations of dependence, in which these healthy drives are subverted into a more grasping, self-centred set of motives. The result of this is unhappiness and moral degradation, perpetuated by unequal and repressive political systems. The society of Rousseau's time, in his view, largely exemplifies this process. If humanity is to escape this situation, then the whole basis on which social relations are conducted will need to be altered. Even if it is impossible to revert back to the state of nature, it may be that there is a way to reconcile the competing demands of people in such a way as to maximize their happiness and fulfilment.

This positive ideal is the project which Rousseau undertakes in *The Social Contract*, to which we now turn.

CHAPTER 3

READING THE TEXT

BOOK I

The ideas Rousseau expounds in *The Social Contract* were originally envisaged as part of a planned larger work to be called 'Political Institutions'. However, Rousseau abandoned his intentions for this more ambitious scheme, and *The Social Contract* remains his most complete work on politics and political philosophy. It is also his most famous and widely read book, the one on which his reputation as a thinker and writer is chiefly based. Despite this, it is relatively short and compact, and much of the important content is compressed into the first two books of the four-book whole. On the surface it is deceptively easy to read, and major ideas are expressed in a concise manner which is refreshingly different from some other more ponderous works of political philosophy. However, this very concision can hide real difficulties in interpretation. As we shall see, it can occasionally be difficult to see what Rousseau means by some of the core terms he advances, even when he himself seems to think their significance must be readily apparent. As a result, there is by no means complete agreement among Rousseau scholars on the best interpretation of such sometimes elliptical ideas. Nonetheless, within the comparatively brief text, there is a wealth of original and provocative thought, much of which continues to exercise political theorists in our own time.

In what follows, the intention is to give a comprehensive overview of the important themes and ideas of *The Social Contract*, as well as an introduction to some of the controversies and difficulties they throw up. As we have seen from a consideration of Rousseau's life and early political writings, the subject of a just and equitable society was never far from his thoughts. His frequent dismay at the problems of his own environment, coupled with his belief in the fundamental goodness of human beings, was the catalyst for positive thoughts about a better form of social organization. In *The Social Contract*, he organizes these thoughts into four books:

1. The fundamentals of a just society and the basic principles of its organization;
2. The legislative framework of the just society;
3. Detail on the various functions and powers of government;
4. Other aspects of social organization, including the place of religion.

Each part is further subdivided in short chapters. By and large, this guide will follow these chapters in sequence, since there is generally a clear chain of reasoning used by Rousseau in developing his arguments. However, not all these sections are as clear as others, nor do all have the same importance in making his case, so we'll spend more time on some sections than others. Each sub-heading in this text will be followed by the corresponding chapter numbers in parentheses, which will make it simple to refer to the relevant parts of the text.

From freedom to chains (1)

As we've seen from our brief look at Rousseau's life, he was familiar with more than one political system. While it was France, a hierarchical monarchy, which provided him with the environment in which he wrote most of his books, republican Geneva was the greater catalyst for his own ideas. On the title page of *The Social Contract*, Rousseau announces himself pointedly as 'a citizen of Geneva'. He also quotes an epigram from Virgil's epic poem *The Aeneid*: *'feoderis aeqas, dicamus leges'* – 'let us make a fair treaty'. These two elements – contemporary republican Geneva and the legacy of an enlightened classical civilization – are the wellsprings of inspiration Rousseau draws on throughout the book. Clearly, despite his pessimism about the corrupting effects of civilization, he thought there were some models worthy of emulation. The imperfect examples provided by Geneva and his readings of classical authors are the basis for much of what he says later.

The next few paragraphs, including the very short first chapter, set out what Rousseau takes to be his task: 'to consider if [. . .] there can be any legitimate and sure principle of government, taking men as they are and laws as they might be' (*SC*, I, 1). The important word here is 'legitimate': Rousseau does not merely wish to establish which of any mechanisms are capable of creating governments; he is interested in which principles create fair and just governments, ones in which the natural goodness of people is not subverted into a destructive form of *amour-propre* or where despotism is possible.

Despite this, he is anxious to avoid pipedreams. His vision for society will be a realistic one (at least in intention). He takes as his starting-point people as they exist – not idealistic versions of them – and then considers what laws and principles may justly govern their lives. With typically refreshing honesty, he claims no unique insight into this issue by virtue of his rank or position (as he remarks, he is neither a prince nor a legislator), but offers up the suggestion that, as a member of a free state with a right to vote, he has a duty to think carefully about the society of which he is a constituent part. As a writer, he has a certain obligation to make a considered contribution to the contest of ideas concerning politics. If he *were* a prince or a legislator, he would be better off putting his ideas into practice rather than spend time theorizing. The idea, casually expressed here, that a right to have a stake in society (in this case, voting on the make-up of the legislative assembly) carries a concomitant obligation to make the best use of it is a simple one, which nonetheless we will see developed in later chapters.

With the preamble out of the way, Rousseau makes one of his most famous and memorable claims: 'Man is born free, and is everywhere in chains' (*SC*, I, 1). This is a characteristically pithy statement of the human predicament we discussed in the previous section. As we know, Rousseau believes that people are by nature benign creatures, free to pursue their natural tendencies for self-preservation and enrichment if left unfettered by external forces. However, poorly formed society tends to corrupt these impulses by encouraging an unhealthy degree of dependence between individuals. Once these relationships of dependence become crystallized and endemic, then the drive of *amour de soi* is replaced by a malign form of *amour-propre*. The 'chains' of the famous phrase are therefore partly psychological. The freedoms originally (and potentially) enjoyed by individuals are stifled by a culture in which it is impossible to get by without resorting to destructive and damaging modes of behaviour.

It is certainly possible to see echoes of Rousseau's own experience in plaintive passages such as these. As we have seen, he was a somewhat brittle character, much given to idealism and flights of imagination, but capable of peevish resentment if he felt his path had been blocked. His own rise to fame from provincial obscurity to the bright lights of the Paris salons was of necessity aided and eased along by characters such as Diderot and the formidable Madame d'Épinay. In time, he came to fall out with almost all of these backers, and saw plots against him multiply from every quarter. In this situation, it must have been easy for Rousseau to see all such relationships of dependence as intrinsically wicked, and to look back on his wandering pre-fame existence as a much more authentic way of living. The freedom of the isolated scholar perhaps contrasted poorly with the pride, vanity and deception he witnessed in Parisian high society. To be forced to exist in such a milieu in order to pursue his goals as a composer and writer seems to have repeatedly struck him as unbearably odious, and as a source of considerable mental disquiet.

The worst folly, for Rousseau, is to believe that one can master the constant battle to negotiate one's way within a society based on interlocking levels of patronage and dependence. Even if one rises to the top, in material terms, there is no escape from the constant need for one's position to be reinforced by others. Those sitting at the apex of the pyramid will be preoccupied with a desire to see their exalted state recognized by those below. Indeed, the very essence of such a state is that it lasts only as long as it is continually and publicly recognized by others, so such people are actually *more* dependent on those beneath them, and are as much prisoners within the system as the unfortunates who have achieved less worldly success.

Of course, there are more straightforward ways of interpreting Rousseau's statement as well. In addition to the psychological chains imposed in poorly constructed societies, there are also more literal varieties: political oppression, slavery and other forms of institutionalized coercion. In an environment where the prevailing drive is malign *amour-propre*, the drive for recognition leads quickly to a state of political inequality. Those who have garnered a greater share of material wealth for themselves will pass laws to protect their gains, while those below will either suffer under the yoke of oppression or somehow fight their way up to a position of power themselves. The passing of laws, and the accompanying institutions which spring up to enforce them, may at first seem like a good way to regulate the competition for resources and prestige which characterizes the dysfunctional social order. The weak, who stand to lose most from a situation where all are at odds with each other, may indeed welcome the provision of regulations, and give up much of their freedom of action in return for the security they think such laws will give them. However, as these laws are principally imposed by those in control, their security is illusory, and the bargain they have secured is a poor one. As Rousseau writes in *The Discourse on the Origin of Inequality,*

> All ran headlong to their chains, in hopes of securing their liberty; for they had just wit enough to perceive the advantages of political institutions, without experience enough to enable them to foresee the dangers. [. . .] Such was, or may well have been, the origin of society and law, which bound new fetters on the poor, and gave new powers to the rich; which irretrievably destroyed natural liberty, eternally fixed the law of property and inequality, converted clever usurpation into unalterable right, and, for the advantage of a few ambitious individuals, subjected all mankind to perpetual labour, slavery, and wretchedness.[1]

This is Rousseau in full, polemic flow, and illustrates the extent of the 'chains' which he thinks bind members of unjust societies. Having sketched such a grim scenario, however, he then confidently claims that he has the solution: a means of turning oppressive political institutions into genuinely legitimate instruments of a benign society. Before moving on to this, though, he spends a few chapters considering the nature of some of the social orders he thought exhibited such destructive features clearly. By exposing their weaknesses, he hopes to bolster the case for his own, reformed political system, the outline of which has yet to be revealed.

Born to rule (2)

Rousseau considers three kinds of unsatisfactory bases for society: authority from nature, the right of the strongest and slavery. To the modern reader, none of these might appear especially promising starting-points for a just political order, and may therefore look like a strange place to start. However, in Rousseau's own time there would have been much more debate about the merits of such forms of governance. Slavery was legal in Europe, and would remain so until the following century. The idea that some groups of people (whether from a particular race, or sex, or even simply from a nation which had established control over others through conquest) were more fitted to rule than others was more intuitively plausible than it may seem today. So Rousseau's targets were not idly chosen. As we shall see later, his own plan for society places great store in the freedom and equality of all its members, so rival accounts based on inherent differences in worth or liberty among individuals or groups are pulling in exactly the opposite direction. Even though it may be difficult to generate much sympathy for the positions he attacks, it is still instructive to follow his reasoning in rejecting them, not least to shed some light on the kinds of criteria Rousseau thought were important when appraising different political systems.

His first target is natural authority. This initially takes the form of an argument by analogy. When we are casting around for a just basis for society, it is natural to look for models in nature. One obvious one is the family. Children do not come into the world as equals with adults. As a matter of survival, they are dependent on the protection of their parents. They are thus naturally subordinate to the head of the household (the father, in Rousseau's description), and have their freedom to do what they want limited in exchange for protection and guidance. To many political theorists of Rousseau's time, such a situation seemed like a helpful example for society too. As such an argument runs, the citizens of the state are like children, the rulers like the father. The rulers derive their right to govern from the same source that the father does in claiming authority over his offspring.

Certainly, it is easy to imagine circumstances where the parallels between familial and state authority are quite close. In feudal societies, for instance, an individual's ability to survive may well have depended on his ability to attach himself to a powerful magnate, in much the same way children are dependent on a father. And the resonance between familial and social relationships is present even in the modern world: one only has to think of religious uses of 'Father' to designate a particular rank or function. In many African languages, the terms 'father' and 'mother' are used as frequently to denote respect and aspects of social hierarchy as they are to pick out family links. As a result of these intuitive similarities, writers such as Robert Filmer had during the seventeenth century extended the analogy fairly systematically, tracing the paternal right of temporal authority back to Adam, and the patriarchal model of politics was well-known and influential.[2]

As Rousseau points out, however, an analogy only shows so much. Just because there are some features in common between the family and the state, it doesn't follow that each should be ordered in the same way, or for the same reasons. After all, there are dissimilarities too. When a child grows up, he or she no longer requires the support of a father, and the natural bond of authority is dissolved. There may still be some lingering relationship of respect and deference, but that is a matter for the individuals involved: a father does not have the same right of authority over an adult son or daughter as over an infant. In addition, a father benefits in a family relationship from the strong feelings of love he feels towards his children. It would be inappropriate, according to Rousseau, for a ruler to feel the same way towards a ruled populace. A good ruler remains impartial towards his subjects; if he did not, his decisions would no doubt lapse into corruption and short-sightedness. As a result of these differences, the family is a poor model for a political system.

These are fairly weak arguments, on both sides. It may be that Rousseau thought the model of the family was a self-evidently poor basis for the state, as his dismissal of it is fairly cursory. However, the appeal of the analogy (should it have any) is really based on the more fundamental idea that there are two separate types of people in the world: those like fathers, who have the power and ability to become rulers, and those like children, who need for their own good to be ruled over and have certain freedoms withdrawn. This notion he considers in slightly more detail, and cites three philosophers – Aristotle, Hobbes and Grotius – as being proponents of views of this kind.

We have already touched briefly on Grotius, to whom Rousseau frequently refers as an intellectual adversary. Grotius was a strong advocate of the rights of rulers over their subjects, and used historical and legal precedent to defend even apparently repressive regimes. Thomas Hobbes, by contrast, argued in favour of strong, authoritarian governments on more practical grounds. Since the state of nature, in his view, was a terrible place of constant warfare between ungoverned individuals (a supposition of exactly the opposite kind to Rousseau's) it is both pragmatic and morally justified for the freedoms of such individuals to be given up to a powerful government. In Hobbes's account, the authority at the head of such a society has sweeping powers to regulate its affairs, and the governed masses relatively little recourse should they dislike the way things are going.[3] In a similar vein, Aristotle argued in his political philosophy that certain classes in society are inherently more suited to rule than others. Some are born for slavery, others to be masters. In a manner reminiscent of the familial analogy, Aristotle argues that some elements of society are simply incapable of making sensible use of complete freedom, and must therefore be guided by those more fitted to the task.[4]

Rousseau rejects the idea that there are inherently two classes of people: those fit to rule and those destined to be ruled. To characterize things in such a way is, for him, similar to describing the ruled as cattle and the rulers as shepherds. It is true that, as a result of custom and tradition, it may *seem* as if some social groups are destined for one fate or another. However, this is to get things the wrong way round. If slaves are held in slavery for long enough, then even they will come to see that as their natural state. Indeed, some may end up thinking it justified, and perhaps take some degree of satisfaction from their lowly station. But that is not because they were fitted to that role prior to society's influence; instead, it is society that has moulded them into the state which only subsequently seems natural for them. We might think of the 'Stockholm Syndrome' phenomenon for an extreme example of this: the tendency some people have to identify with their oppressors even in very stressful and abusive situations.

Rousseau's argument against a natural hierarchy of groups within society is very brief. It may seem as if he has given hardly any attention to it. However, it is worth bearing in mind here our earlier discussion of human nature and psychology. In Rousseau's reading of them, Aristotle and his ilk assume that people have a certain set of capacities *before* entering the social order, and the state should organize itself around those differing capacities. However, for Rousseau, society itself is responsible for altering people's basic psychology and motivations. The point of making his suppositions about the state of nature is partly to make this notion clear. And if that account is at all persuasive, then it is consistent of him to reject the notion that certain groups within society ought, from the very beginning, to be accorded more rights than others. For him, the apparent suitability of some for slavery and others for finery is a *symptom* of an unjust society, not a reason for its establishment. The idea that there is an inherent hierarchy among people, the rulers and the ruled, is mistaken therefore because it relies on a distorted view of human nature. After all, in the imagined pre-civilized state there are no rulers: it is only the development of dysfunctional societies which divides the human race into such classes.

So, in Rousseau's view, the fitness (or otherwise) of certain classes of people is the product of a social order, rather than a justification for it. In other words, it is nurture, not nature, which determines who become rulers and who becomes ruled. And at least as far as social groups or classes go, Rousseau's views are very much in sympathy with those of our own time. There have of course been many theories aiming to show that certain groups are more or less suited to positions of authority or freedom than others. At various points in history it has seemed quite acceptable to argue that a certain social class, race or sex is naturally superior to another, and by virtue of such superiority ought to have more freedom or power than another. There are few today who would make such an argument. It is a matter of some debate, of course, whether different sexes or races have sufficient genetic distinctiveness of a relevant kind to enable *some* conclusions to be drawn about their prospects or abilities. But the terrible consequences of making pseudo-scientific judgements about race during the twentieth century, combined with the long process of granting civil rights to women and ethnic minorities in the Western world have generally, and surely rightly, led to the rejection of social theories based on certain groups having an inherent right and duty to rule. So, even if his arguments against such a position are somewhat hasty, Rousseau is certainly advocating a position which the modern reader is likely to accept.

Might is right (3)

Having rejected a social order based on natural authority, Rousseau turns to a simpler form of unsuitable government: the right of the strongest. Here the position might be something like this: even if there are no classes of people who are inherently suited to govern, perhaps we should simply accept that whoever is strong enough to accumulate power to themselves should be in charge. If there are no pre-existing groups which obviously have the necessary attributes to govern, then the leader with sufficient might to dominate his or her counterparts is the best candidate. In such a scenario, it would be perfectly reasonable for citizens to give up their freedoms to whichever tyrant manages to defeat all comers – indeed, they would hardly have any choice in the matter. And such a state of affairs is not something to be resisted, but a perfectly natural and proper way of organizing things.

Rousseau gives this idea even shorter shrift. He starts off by observing that no-one, not even the mightiest ruler, could rule by force all the time. If a ruler is to have time to do anything other than put down rebellions, then they need to have at least some degree of acquiescence from their subjects. And this means getting some of them to accept, at least some of the time, that the rule of force is not only a fact of life, but somehow justified as well. For Rousseau, though, the idea that there can be a 'right' to government by the strongest is nonsense. What does this right consist in? The very idea of rule by the strongest is inimical to the idea of rights. Suppose a ruler at some point loses the ability to control his subjects, and they successfully depose him. He cannot appeal to the right of the strongest, since he is no longer capable of imposing his will by strength. Whoever successfully usurps the position can invoke such a 'right' themselves, but that does no more than assert the factual position that they are now the more powerful. In other words, the 'right' of the strongest is just another way for those who have actually achieved power to justify their actions after the event. It has no explanatory or moral force: the doctrine of 'might makes right' has zero power to persuade citizens that such rule is legitimate or justified. An individual may be compelled by necessity to accept the rule of someone stronger than they are, but they are never forced by reason to do so. As Rousseau remarks, if an armed robber holds him up he may have to give up his belongings to stay alive, but if he can somehow keep them hidden then he has every justification to try.

This point is important, because Rousseau is only interested in establishing what kind of social order is *legitimate*. He does not primarily concern himself with other criteria of success, such as material or technological advancement. If he did, then perhaps the rule of the strongest may have some appeal. It is possible to imagine a situation where an iron fist may be required to achieve some important social goal, and where questions of legitimacy may seem at least temporarily more important. In recent history, one might argue that only a monstrous dictator such as Stalin could have successfully defended his country from invasion in World War II and dragged such a vast and disparate nation into the industrial age. In such circumstances, a social order which depended on some kind of legitimacy in its affairs may not have been able to survive. So, arguably, there are at least some occasions where rule by the strongest is justifiable, and where citizens may be rational to acquiesce to that rule. But, for Rousseau, this is to miss the point. There may always be *some* benefits in rule by the strongest over, say, rule by no-one at all. Indeed, virtually any system of government is likely to have advantages over complete anarchy (even Rousseau thought that competition for scarce resources was capable of turning the benign state of nature into a Hobbesian free-for-all, as we'll see later). But, as we have seen already, the development of technology, arts, sciences or material prosperity is of secondary importance to Rousseau – he is primarily looking for a social means to safeguard human equality and freedom. So even if rule by the strongest may, arguably, bring some practical benefits, it cannot ground the kind of legitimate society which is the target of his enquiry.

Slavery (4)

Having dismissed the ideas of natural authority and the rule of the strongest, Rousseau concludes that the only basis for a just society is one founded on a covenant: an agreement between all members of the society to live under rules they all agree on.

In what comes later, he will outline the exact form of covenant which he feels generates the optimal political order. Before that, however, he feels compelled to dismiss an alternative version. The inspiration for the discussion comes, once again, from Grotius, who claims that 'a people may give itself to a king'. In other words, the covenant may take the form of a populace deciding to give up their freedom to an individual who will then rule over them. Rousseau considers perhaps the most extreme example of this, which is slavery. He begins the chapter by considering whether a covenant of this sort provides a more satisfactory basis for society than those already discussed. He also discusses a slightly different case: whether enslaving a population as a result of a war between rival states can ever be justified. Unsurprisingly, both questions are answered in the negative. Some of the reasons he gives, however, develop a little further the psychological background we have already covered.

Rousseau begins by asking whether it makes any sense for a person to sell his or her freedom to another in exchange for other benefits (say, security or material well-being). Suppose an individual lost all their possessions in some disaster. They may be able to sell the only thing they have left – themselves – to another in order to secure food and shelter. Or it may be the case, more generally, that there are advantages to be had in swapping freedom for protection and ownership. Rousseau is not having any of this. His principal objection is with the notion of *what* is being given away. A person cannot give up their very essence – freedom – without in some sense ceasing to exist as a proper moral entity. In such a case, they have alienated themselves from the human qualities which underpin the covenant itself. It ceases to be an agreement between two people, properly understood, and becomes a relationship of pure force. Understood thus, it is no different from the right of the strongest, even if the origin of the arrangement may have been voluntary. As with the rule of the strongest, slavery may in some cases bring certain material benefits, but it fails the test of being truly based on a covenant – for that to be the case, both parties must come together in some sense as individuals of a comparable moral level. The fact that the slave-owner *possesses* the other participant in the deal renders the deal void.

In addition to this argument based on a conception of human nature, Rousseau also has more practical objections to slavery. He considers Grotius's idea of an individual or a people exchanging their freedom in exchange for other benefits, such as security. For Rousseau, it is just as likely that the despotism which emerges as a result of this exchange would be as bad as the insecure state which the slave originally wished to avoid. Once a ruler gains absolute rights over his subjects, there can be no guarantee that the consequences for the ruled won't be worse than the state they chose to escape. Indeed, the lesson of history shows that conditions are likely to be fairly miserable. In addition, the idea of an entire people giving itself up to slavery poses its own problems. What happens when the children of those slaves mature into adults? Will they have to renegotiate the covenant? If so, then the idea of a ruler gaining absolute rights over his subjects is undermined, since the ruled will constantly be demanding fresh covenants. If the ruler insists that the children of slaves fall under the terms of the original covenant, then this removes any pretence that it is a genuine, voluntary agreement. In sum, it is not possible to generate a social order based on slavery which genuinely derives from a covenant. Either the slavery is real, in which case the covenant is void and it is really rule by the strongest, or else the covenant is real, in which case the parties to it cannot include slaves.

Rousseau also discusses the idea that a victorious army may be justified in enslaving a conquered populace. The length of time he spends considering this is slightly puzzling, given how much more intuitively unacceptable it seems even than the previous account of slavery. However, at the time of his writing, the idea that there was legitimacy in sparing the lives of enemy combatants in order to enslave them was (partly thanks to our friend Grotius) certainly not as outlandish as it may strike us today. Rousseau therefore takes some care to establish that wars are properly the purview of states, rather than affairs between individuals, and that the rules of war, as applied to states, are in force. These dictate that enemy combatants who have laid down their arms may not be killed. So there can be no legitimate bargain in which liberty is exchanged for life, since the victor has no right to force such terms on the vanquished. Should these principles be violated, then the imposition of slavery is simply a reiteration of the right of the strongest once more. And this is surely right: even if one were to quibble with Rousseau's assertion that the conduct of war is always a matter for states, or that this is even a relevant point to make, it seems hard to argue that the forced slavery practised by victorious armies is anything other than a most egregious example of the 'might is right' doctrine already considered and rejected.

By the end of Chapter 5 of Book I, then, Rousseau has marshalled some persuasive arguments against a social order based on the voluntary (or involuntary) relinquishing of freedom to an all-powerful authority. One of the powerful ideas expressed in this section – that a just social order may only comprise individuals of an equal moral standing and significance – will be developed and expanded upon in what is to come. And yet, even if it is easy to agree with him about the unacceptability of slavery, we may have some doubts over whether Rousseau has properly considered more reasonable versions of the idea that a society can opt to hand over significant freedoms in a covenant for their own benefit. An example of such a position is Thomas Hobbes's, who despite Rousseau's rather cavalier dismissal at the start of this discussion expounds a more nuanced authoritarian position than his reputation sometimes suggests.

In Hobbes's view, as we have briefly noted, the state of nature is a terrible place. If not carefully managed by a sufficiently powerful central authority, the scarcity and uncertainty of natural resources foments endless conflict, destroying any lasting prospect of material progress or spiritual wellbeing. Accordingly, he argues, it is in the populace's interest to sign over a large portion of their freedom to a powerful sovereign so that their affairs may be regulated more fairly and predictably. In exchange for losing certain liberties, the people gain the civil peace to go about their lawful business, to the benefit of all. As in Rousseau's account, the idea is that the populace enters into a covenant with each other to hand over rights to a powerful sovereign: they decide that they are better off losing their unfettered capacity to act in favour of a generally more beneficial social environment. In Hobbes's exposition of these ideas, the sovereign authority accrues an impressive range of powers, such as control of the press, the military and the passing of laws. The subjects of such an authority may not legally change their form of government, even if they find it oppressive and cruel (though the sovereign does have, in Hobbes's view, powerful reasons for acting in a generally beneficent way). As he says,

> A commonwealth is said to be instituted, when a multitude of men do agree, and covenant, every one, with every one, [. . .] the right to present the person of them all (that is to say, to be their representative) [such that they may] live peaceably amongst themselves, and be protected against other men. [. . .] From this institution of a commonwealth are derived all the rights, and faculties of him, or them, on whom sovereign power is conferred by the consent of the people assembled. [. . .] There can happen no breach of covenant on the part of the sovereign; and consequently none of his subjects, by any pretence of forfeiture, can be freed from his subjection.[5]

The precise details and potential difficulties of Hobbes's account need not detain us. The point in raising it is that there may be some form of contractual arrangement in which individual freedoms are given up to a powerful authority, but which falls short of outright slavery. If such an account could be constructed, it would avoid some of Rousseau's counter-arguments, especially those which depend on the idea that slaves cannot be proper parties to a covenant. Once again, there is a parallel here with the feudal model, in which there is an explicit link between the loyalty owed by peasant workers to their Lord and his ability to protect them against attack. Hobbes himself was greatly influenced by the example of the English Civil War, where it seemed to him that having a very powerful monarchy was preferable to the alternative of chaos and warfare. Even if such a view is authoritarian, it is certainly not obviously or inevitably a recipe for slavery.

So, in considering alternatives to his own, yet to be announced theory, is Rousseau guilty of the 'straw man' fallacy: setting up implausible rival theories and ignoring better versions in order that his own account may appear superior? To some extent, yes. If Rousseau's purpose in listing the weaknesses of alternative political models was to eliminate all other possibilities but his own, then he has left potential gaps. However, it would be very difficult to reject every possible variation of an authoritarian or non-covenantal political theory, and, in a relatively brief work such as *The Social Contract*, probably counter-productive. After all, there is a limit to how persuasive it is to list the defects of political models in the hope of settling on something else by default.

So, being a little charitable, we might view Rousseau's strategy in the following light: in the opening chapters, he has considered and rejected some influential theories of social organization (at least in his own time), and in such a way as to limit the remaining possibilities. He has not dismissed every permutation of these theories by any means, but he has used his rejection of them to enhance the acceptability of two core notions: that a legitimate society is based on some form of covenant, and that the quality of freedom is essential if the participants in the covenant are to count as genuine partners. In the following three chapters, these notions are given some concrete shape. As we shall see then, a Hobbesian-type society such as the one we have sketched here would be incompatible with Rousseau's account, since it turns out that *any* diminution of an individual's freedom in favour of another is rejected. To see how this radical idea will be developed, we will have to turn now from Rousseau's negative views on rival political philosophies to the positive exposition of his own.

A social pact (5–6)

In Chapters 5 and 6, Rousseau outlines in a very compressed way his vision for a just and legitimate society. As is typical, major ideas are introduced very quickly, and often with great rhetorical force. The advantage of this approach is that, in a short space of time, Rousseau outlines a great deal of his political model, and we can readily gain an impression of the entire shape of his project. The disadvantage is that some of the key concepts he employs remain under-developed. In fact, some central notions are only ever fully elucidated in a piecemeal fashion across several chapters of *The Social Contract*. So when reading these two chapters, it should be borne in mind that there is further development of the key ideas to come, and that some puzzling features of his account do receive more detailed treatment later in the book.

Rousseau starts with a preamble on the need, once again, for an original covenant. He develops a point made earlier on the balance of power between a master and slaves, and argues that such an unequal relationship is an empty and pointless one. If the basis of a social order is derived from force, then there is no proper bond of rational obligation between the ruled and the rulers. Though the populace of such a state may be compelled to obey the laws of their master, the resultant situation does not merit the term 'political association', since there is no legitimate basis for the arrangement. Should the bonds of force dissolve at any point, through death or insurrection, then nothing would be left of the institutions themselves. As a final parting shot at Grotius (for now), he attacks the idea that the act of a people giving themselves up to a monarch forms the fundamental instance of a political association. If 'the people' are acting together in such a way as to decide to surrender their freedom to an individual, then they must have already come together in some form of political group, which presumably involves some kind of prior binding agreement. In other words, the covenant which shapes the social order is already in place, and the presence of a monarch is a subsequent (and unwelcome) feature of the political order.

The point about priority is perhaps not very important, and indeed sits rather uneasily with some of the things Rousseau says later. There *are* some practical issues concerning the precise means by which a population can enter into a social contract, but we'll look at them in some detail later on. The main thing to note here is that, for Rousseau, the covenant is the essential first ingredient in a well-ordered society. Only this approach holds out the promise that the resultant community will cultivate the flourishing of human potential and freedom. But, as we have seen, there are potential covenants which are in his view contradictory or unacceptable. What is the distinctive feature of Rousseau's own account?

Rousseau starts by reminding us of the conditions which lead people out of the state of nature. At some point in human history, he claims, sufficient obstacles to the preservation of the species present themselves so that there are material and prudential reasons for associating in ever greater numbers. He does not expand on what those obstacles might be, but following Hobbes's account, we could assume that he means something like scarcity of resources, or the threat of natural disasters. By uniting their practical abilities, groups of people are more effective than lone individuals in responding to such challenges. Indeed, conglomerations of this kind are probably essential to the survival of the species, since the dangers posed by the natural world are significant and deadly. (This passage is further evidence that Rousseau did not think a return to a state of nature was possible, despite its beneficial effects on humanity's psychological wellbeing.) As we have seen, however, the potential for disaster is high in such a scenario. The natural tendency for people to maintain their own interests presents a clear potential for clashes. It is very likely that the various motivations to preserve individual livelihoods will come into conflict, especially if essential resources are scarce and the actions of the group are lightly regulated. In the worst case, affairs degenerate into a condition worse than the perilous state of nature itself: a brutal anarchy, or the imposition of the kind of repressive authority which has already been rejected. What is needed is a form of organization which guarantees the security and interests of its constituents while also preserving their freedom and wellbeing. As Rousseau puts it, the question is this:

> How to find a form of association which will defend the person and goods of each member with the collective force of all, and under which each individual, while uniting himself with others, obeys no-one but himself, and remains as free as before. (*SC*, I, 6)

A difficult-looking task, but one which Rousseau feels he has the answer to. He goes on to claim that the nature of his envisaged social covenant is such that its benefits and obligations will be obvious to everyone. If the terms of the covenant are ever violated, even in the smallest degree, then the contract becomes null and void, and the populace immediately revert to whatever system they were living under previously.

Rousseau's central idea is then elucidated:

> These articles of association, rightly understood, are reducible to a single one, namely the total alienation by each associate of himself and all his rights to the whole community. Thus [. . .] as every individual gives himself absolutely, the conditions are the same for all, and precisely because they are the same for all, it is in no-one's interest to make the conditions onerous for others. (*SC*, I, 6)

On a first reading, this 'solution' seems utterly bizarre. How can a social model where everybody gives up *all* their rights possibly render the constituents 'as free as before'? Is this not just as monstrous as the society based on slavery? Some critics of Rousseau have indeed thought so. But before we jump to such a conclusion, we need to pay attention to the stated differences between this account and those which have gone before. The first point to make is that in this scheme, an individual does not give up his or her freedom to another individual, as is the case between a master and a slave. The potential citizen of Rousseau's state gives up their freedom to the community as a whole. No other member of that community, whatever role they may play, has a greater purchase on the freedom given up than any other. Second, everyone in the community has made the same sacrifice. No-one retains a greater level of freedom than anyone else, so there are no comparative winner and losers when it comes to liberty. Because everybody loses all of their rights, and all are thus on the same level, no-one has any reason to propose or pass onerous or unfair laws and regulations. So the community has a safeguard against degenerating into the despotism Rousseau is so opposed to.

Such is the key starting point of Rousseau's political order. Immediately, we are likely to want to ask more questions. How exactly does this contractual arrangement work? And how can it possibly guarantee meaningful freedom if everyone loses *all* their rights to everyone else? Over the next few chapters, Rousseau does attempt to give an answer to both questions. But from the start he faces something of a conceptual problem. Earlier he stated that an agreement between two parties where one loses all their freedom and the other retains theirs was no sort of agreement at all: a proper convention requires both participants to retain a full and rounded moral personality. How is this situation different? Apart from the claim that, in the latter case, the individual is contracting with an abstract entity (the community) rather than another individual, it looks rather like the terms of the contract are just as null and void as those in the earlier case, since all those signing up for it lose their entire body of rights and privileges. In fact, as Rousseau will later claim, his form of covenant actually results in every member of the community *enhancing* their freedom, despite appearances. The reasons for this are fairly complex, and rely on an understanding of Rousseau's conception of the best kind of freedom. We'll look at this properly below in our discussion of the benefits of civil society. For now, though, we should note that Rousseau is alive to this objection, and believes that when his entire theory has been laid-out, the sense in which people become *more* free by giving up all their individual liberty will become obvious.

In the meantime, he spends some time to emphasize that his vision for the community really does involve the complete renunciation of rights and privileges to the whole. There are no exceptions or extenuating conditions: once an individual has partaken of *The Social Contract*, they are bound by it utterly. After all, if rights were left to individuals to determine, then each would naturally attempt to accumulate more than their neighbour, and the pernicious competition and patronage of the tyrannical society would reassert itself. However, the participants should not feel alarmed by this absolute condition of association. Since they do not give their rights to any one person, they need not fear that they will be abused by anyone else. In Rousseau's formulation, by giving themselves to everyone, they give themselves to no-one. And as everyone else is in the same situation, no-one has any interest in turning the community into a repressive state. If they did, they would be subjecting themselves to despotism.

At this stage, it should be clear enough that, if it could be realized, Rousseau's radical model does avoid at least some of the salient negative features of the other societies he has considered and rejected. In the sketchy form we have at present, it is already obvious that there is little space for an individual dictator to take control. As there are no distinctions between any members of the community in terms of rights and freedoms, there isn't a natural foothold for a tyrant to base a claim to authority on. And in a situation where everyone's individual rights are exactly the same, if it could be realized, then the emergence of the factions and patronage which Rousseau so despised has correspondingly little purchase. But as yet we have no idea of how such a radical contract would work, or whether, once established, it would achieve the results Rousseau hopes. As he develops the model over the following chapters, it is therefore useful to keep two criteria in mind:

1. Is the model coherent and conceptually sound? Can the central ideas be expressed clearly with no ambiguity or contradiction?
2. If so, what would be the practical consequences of such a society? Most importantly, would it really deliver the benefits Rousseau desires: freedom for all, and the flourishing of human potential?

We'll see, as we progress, that there are a number of points where the satisfaction of both criteria is questionable. But for now we should allow Rousseau a little more space to flesh out the bones of his proposal, before returning to assess how plausible it is.

The sovereign (7)

Rousseau concludes his introduction of the social pact with a rather confusing list of distinctions and definitions. The two most important for us are his use of the terms *state* and *sovereign*, which are essential in understanding how, in practical terms, his community is intended to regulate itself. So far, all we know is that the genesis of Rousseau's community is an agreement by everyone to relinquish their rights to the rest, taken as a whole. Once this has happened, the question of how decisions will subsequently be made immediately arises. No-one is obviously in charge, and if the manifest dangers and challenges of the natural world are to be met, there must be some way of establishing good policies and regulations. Rousseau's answer, logically enough, is that everyone in the community makes the decisions. The resolutions of the community are binding on all because they are made by all. So each member is at once (a) subject to the laws of the community and is also (b) an architect of them. When Rousseau uses the term 'state' he is referring to the former condition of the community: its passive role as an entity subject to laws. When he uses the terms 'sovereign' he means the latter condition: its active role as the decision-making body in the community:

> Each person, in making a contract, as it were, with himself, finds himself doubly committed, first, as a member of the sovereign

body in relation to individuals, and secondly as a member of the
state in relation to the sovereign. (*SC*, I, 7)

Rousseau spends some time explaining the advantages of such a
system. According to him, it ensures that the sovereign power will be
obliged to pursue policies for the benefit of all, for two main reasons.
First, the sovereign owes its existence to *The Social Contract*, in which
all its constituents have the same share. To violate the position of any
individual within the community would be to violate that contract,
and hence dissolve the sovereign power itself. When the sovereign
acts, it must do so in accordance with the contract from which its
power derives. Second, as the sovereign is composed of all members
of the community, it will have no motivation to harm them. Using a
common political analogy, Rousseau points out that it is impossible
for a body to harm all of its members.

Stated baldly thus, it all may seem rather too good to be true. It is
certainly possible to imagine a community in which the decisions are
taken by an assembly of all its members. But surely, one might argue,
given human fallibility and moral failing, it would soon degenerate
into factional interests or classes. Even if decisions are made by
everyone with an equal share in the process, what is to stop a majority coming together to dominate the proceedings? Or individuals
deciding that their own private interests are more important than
the wellbeing of everyone else? These are obvious objections, and
Rousseau is fully aware of them. His response to the first problem,
that of the sovereign power being dominated by a majority faction, is
dealt with in the next book (*SC*, II, 2–3) and so we will discuss the
somewhat surprising implications of his views on that later. But the
issue of individual preferences asserting themselves is addressed right
away, and in considering how to deal with this issue, Rousseau introduces one of his most important and difficult concepts.

He starts by acknowledging that, naturally, everyone has a private
interest, and there is no guarantee that this will correspond to the
general good. In fact, it is very unlikely to do so with any great regularity – there will be many occasions where an individual will be
better off, at least temporarily, by pursuing a course of action contrary to the interests of the rest of the community. In economics,
such a situation is often referred to as the 'tragedy of the commons':
where resources are held in common, there is always an incentive for
an individual to seize more than their fair share, even if that results

in long-term shortages for everyone. However, Rousseau also argues that each individual also has a 'general will', insofar as they are a citizen of the state. The idea of the 'general will' is one of the most perplexing ideas in the entire *Social Contract*, even though it is essential to the coherence of the whole. Frustratingly, there is no one part of the treatise where the notion is comprehensively elucidated. In Book II, however, there is a much more sustained discussion of what kind of thing the general will must be, and how it functions as a regulator of the sovereign's activities. For now, though, we can accept a rather rough-and-ready definition of it: the general will, as it applies to individuals, is the motivation to do what is in the interests of the community as a whole, as opposed to what is in the interests of the individual themselves. So even though all the members of the sovereign no doubt have their own private desires and wants, Rousseau claims that there is also an impersonal general will which must be followed. If everyone does this, then the sovereign will always govern the community in a just and impartial manner.

If the vision of a harmonious sovereign body acting in the interests of all seemed too good to be true earlier, then this initial response is unlikely to make things much better. We have been told that there is a thing called the 'general will', which individuals possess and can be aware of, and that if the sovereign acts in accordance with it, then all shall be well. It is all still very speculative, and, one might also think, rather optimistic. In fact, as we shall discover, Rousseau *does* have some reasons for supposing that a sovereign will have a pressure exerted on it to act as a singular entity for the benefit of the whole community, and much more to say about the workings of the general will. Again, we will see these reasons made a little more clear in Book II. But even now, with only the sketchiest knowledge of the general will and its operation, we are still left with our original objection: what happens if, despite knowledge of the general will and the consequences of acting against it, an individual still opts to pursue a private interest, even when constituting a part of an active sovereign power?

Here, Rousseau makes one of his most infamous moves. He claims straightaway that if an individual persists in a course of action in contradiction to the general will, then they will be constrained to fall into line by the whole of the rest of the sovereign body. In his own rather chilling formula, he announces that the recusant will 'be forced to be free'. In practical terms, this means that they will be compelled to act in accordance with the decision of the entire community. It is

certainly hard to see how this squares with his original objective: to
come up with a form of political association which provides security
while still preserving as much freedom as an individual has in the
state of nature. From the discussion so far, it may well seem that
nothing of the sort has been achieved, and Rousseau has done no
more than create a whole community of slaves, all of whom have
derogated their rights to a vague and nebulous 'general will', the basis
of which is still very unclear. Indeed, this might seem even worse
than a society based on natural authority or force of the strongest,
since at least in those scenarios *some* people retained their freedom to
act in their own best interests. If Rousseau's account is to strike us as
all coherent and credible, then we should want to know a lot more
about the workings of the general will. Likewise, if he is to convince
us that his system meets the goal of guaranteeing freedom and human
flourishing, then we should want to hear more about how being
'forced' to act in accordance with the will of the sovereign could con-
tribute to that objective.

Thankfully for us, Rousseau does say more about each issue. The
first chapters of Book II contain more detail on the general will and
how it is discovered and acted on, but he first spends a little time discussing his particular conception of freedom, to which we now turn.

Real freedom (8)

Should things be ordered in the way Rousseau suggests, he claims
that the transition into civil society from the state of nature has precisely the opposite effect to that outlined earlier in our discussion of
poorly constructed political systems. Instead of corrupting people's
inherent goodness, civil society enhances the best human qualities
and enables its citizens to live lives of greater moral purpose and
significance. For Rousseau, the change is quite profound: transformed from a creature of simple instinct and narrow outlook, the
citizen is capable of acting in accordance with higher concepts, such
as duty and responsibility. These are real practical benefits: in
exchange for the loss of freedom at an individual level, parties to *The
Social Contract* gain the ability to think and act at a more elevated
level. Instead of being a slave to their appetites, forever concerned by
the prospect of the next meal or a threat to the possessions they may
have accumulated, citizens of a well-run society are able to concen-
trate on the greater good, and turn their mind to projects of more

profound and lasting benefit. In doing so, their lives become more significant, and freer, than they would have done otherwise.

Here then are some initial reasons why Rousseau's state, by his own account, succeeds in guaranteeing human freedoms despite the apparently draconian powers of the sovereign. Once again, in order to make this plausible, we must bear in mind the psychological under-pinnings to his social theory. To recall, Rousseau believes that the quality of compassion plays a privileged role in human dealings. A psychologically healthy individual will be motivated by a benign self-interest modified by a natural desire to help others when they are suffering. Only when such instincts are perverted by poorly con-structed societies does this urge become subsumed by the strident demands of malign *amour-propre*, and beneficent self-interest turns into malignant self-love. When the possibility of providing mutual assistance to our fellow citizen is dimmed by the pressures of ubiqui-tous selfishness and patronage, our moral imagination becomes limited, and we are increasingly subject to an inward-looking desire to please ourselves. Though our actions may be unconstrained by any external force, a more satisfying and significant mode of living has been denied us. As a result, we are less free, and the opportunity to fulfil our true human potential has been taken away.

Though we are as yet still waiting for a more precise account of how Rousseau's ideal community wards against these dangers, it should be at least reasonably evident in which direction his thought is headed. Since in his civil society every decision is made by all mem-bers, and is also binding on all members, there is a clear reason for each individual to think about how their actions bear on the entire community. As there will never be a case where a citizen can pass laws which only affect other people, each will be more inclined to consider the broader implications of any proposal. By doing so, they will bind themselves more closely with the interests of the entire group, rather than sticking slavishly to their own. Presumably, the beneficial effects of thinking in such a way will become increasingly apparent as time goes on and the community flourishes. It is there-fore perfectly proper that dissenters from the general decisions of the group should be bound to accept the sovereign's will, since they are but part of a project which holds the promise of ennobling and uplifting all of its members. In time, even they might come to recog-nize the enormous benefits of being part of such an association, even if in the short term their individual will has been frustrated.

If one is sympathetic to Rousseau's general views on psychological health and the proper motives of humankind, then this position may be an attractive one. But it is still far from certain that his account satisfies our earlier worries about an over-mighty sovereign power. An objector might reason as follows. We have been told that the objective of Rousseau's social order is to guarantee each constituent's freedom to the same level as it was prior to the beginning of the political association. Now we have been presented with an outline of such a society in which any voices dissenting from the opinion of the entire community are silenced. Even if we accept that such a political system may bring some genuine benefits to its members, it still doesn't guarantee *freedom*, since any opinion contrary to that of the general will is suppressed. Whatever good things the dissenting citizen may have gained by being party to *The Social Contract*, they have not retained their liberty, since this has been entirely given away to the will of the sovereign. Thus, Rousseau's system fails in achieving its key criterion of success.

Of course, Rousseau believes his account not only protects freedom, but actually enhances it. So it looks very much as though he and the objector are talking at cross purposes, and that what they have in mind by the term 'freedom' must be rather different. And it turns out that Rousseau does make an important distinction near the end of this chapter between 'natural liberty', which is the kind one has in the state of nature, and 'civil liberty', which is what he has in mind. It is the latter sort which is always in accordance with the general will, and which the citizen of his state gains at the expense of their natural freedom. So when Rousseau claims his society preserves freedom, he is thinking of 'civil liberty', and when he accepts the case of a community forcing a member to accord with the general will, this is on the basis that only 'natural liberty' is violated.

Frustratingly, Rousseau says relatively little further to justify and explain this important difference, claiming at the end of the chapter to have already said enough on the matter. But we can perhaps do some more to make his aims clearer by appealing to a pair of concepts often used in political philosophy. In 1958, Isaiah Berlin wrote a famous paper entitled 'Two Concepts of Liberty'.[6] He argued that there were two competing ideas of freedom, which he termed 'negative' and 'positive'. The former is the simplest, and perhaps most intuitive: negative freedom is just the absence of external restraint on an individual's actions. A person is (negatively) free if they are able to carry out what they wish to do at any given time. If they are prevented from doing so, for any reason, then their liberty has been taken away. Now, there may still be many instances when it is right for a political power to restrict such negative freedom. If someone wanted to murder people indiscriminately, then there would be plenty of justification for curtailing their freedom to act. However, in such a case, there would be no claim that the act of curtailing the murderer *enhances* their freedom; instead, it is accepted that in some cases an individual's freedom should be limited. In the absence of extenuating circumstances, negative freedom is a something to be protected and encouraged, but there may be limits to this if the benefits of freedom impede other social goods, such as personal security. A classically liberal position, using the notion of negative freedom, might be constructed along the lines that an individual should be free to do what they wish, so long as their actions do not lead to others being directly harmed.

It is clear that, at least in the rough form articulated here, Rousseau's political system does not guarantee negative freedom thus construed. *The Social Contract* dictates that each member gives up their individual right to act as they choose in favour of the general will of the community. The sovereign may choose to coerce any one of its members *just if* the member has a divergent view from the general will. In addition, Rousseau argues that such a state of affairs is consistent with the freedom of every individual in the community being enhanced, rather than diminished. His position is much closer therefore to Berlin's idea of 'positive' freedom. Here, the central idea is that an individual is more (positively) free the more opportunities they have to enhance their life and pursue objectives which lead to beneficial outcomes. A good society should act to ensure that its citizens have as wide and as healthy a range of choices as it can. According to the proponent of positive freedom, it is insufficient simply to remove unnecessary constraints from an individual; instead, they should be helped to take advantage of potentially beneficial situations they might otherwise have no access to. A commonplace example is that of forcing children to go to school. Much of the time, children would prefer not to be in the classroom, and if unconstrained by rules and the threat of punishment would probably opt to go elsewhere. But if they were allowed to do this whenever they chose, their opportunities in later life would be severely curtailed: they might lose the freedom to pursue a good career due to a lack of skills, and be confined to a lifestyle with very limited choices. For a supporter of positive freedom, the act of making a child go to school can therefore be seen as enhancing their total liberty, despite the fact it involves placing limits on their actions.

Rousseau is generally seen as one of the chief proponents of positive freedom, and his 'civil liberty' is certainly closer to this idea than it is to Berlin's notion of negative freedom. For this reason his philosophy is often criticized by those of a classically liberal persuasion. Berlin's own paper was sceptical of societies based on the idea of maximizing positive freedom, on the grounds that it leads to overbearing governments, ever ready to interfere with their subjects' lives. Even if such governments' intentions are good, and the authorities genuinely wish to help their citizens move in the right directions, who is to say that their judgement will be better than the citizens'? In any case, such societies will likely tend towards repression and totalitarianism, since individuals will have no protection against the government acting against their interests – everything is being done, after all, to maximize *their* freedom.

Does Rousseau's social order fall into this category of totalitarianism? Certainly, many have thought so. In making up our own minds, however, we might want to have rather more information than we currently do on the precise role and activities of the sovereign. Is there anything in Rousseau's account, for example, which would prevent the sovereign over-reaching itself and becoming a repressive authority? Is there any reason for thinking that, as implied, the general will always point the best way forward for the community? If so, how can it be known with certainty? These are difficult questions for Rousseau, and he does take time to address them. As mentioned earlier, however, these issues are worked-through more thoroughly in Book II, so we should defer a discussion on the coherence and acceptability of his scheme until then. For now, we will have to rest content with the brief positive explanation of civil freedom he offers, and hope that the obvious worries about such a position are addressed when he comes to outline the nature of the general will, and the nature of the sovereign power, in more detail.

Before moving on to that, though, we might consider one practical reason why Rousseau must insist that the sovereign is justified in compelling non-conformists to fall into line. As we have seen, the sovereign body is made up of all the citizens within the state. There is no question of some members dropping out from time to time.

The essential and distinctive feature of Rousseau's model is that all these individuals are in the same boat: all make the laws, and all have the laws applied to them equally. While this condition is sustained, his community is clearly of a different kind to the others we have considered (those where one group makes the laws, and others have them imposed on them). If there is even the possibility of an individual opting out of Rousseau's social contract, then it is not hard to see the entire project unravelling in short order. The freedom, however limited, for a person to exercise a partial will in contradiction to the general will would mean Rousseau's grand hope – that people would move from considering themselves as a set of disconnected individuals to seeing themselves as equal partners in a shared project – will never be realized. For the 'remarkable change in man' which he advocates to take place, it is therefore important that all are compelled to go along with the project. Without such compulsion, the model loses its unique feature, and the possibility of success.

Property (9)

Before moving on to his more detailed discussion of the powers of the sovereign and the nature of the general will, Rousseau spends a little time to outline how the notion of property functions in his ideal community. That he does so just after his account of civil freedom is no accident: for many theorists both before and after Rousseau, the concepts of liberty and property go very closely together. The right to own property is seen by some as a fundamental pillar of freedom, and by others as a tool for oppression and inequality. In Rousseau's argument, the nature of property is somewhat parallel to the nature of freedom. In the same way that an individual moves from an unsatisfactory 'natural liberty' in the state of nature to a fulfilling 'civil liberty' via *The Social Contract*, they move from simply having 'possessions' in the state of nature to obtaining a genuine form of legal property in the civil state, backed by the underwriting power of the sovereign. The way in which Rousseau thinks this works, given his earlier insistence that every individual gives up all their rights to everyone else in *The Social Contract*, is somewhat complex.

He starts by re-emphasizing that when a person enters *The Social Contract*, they give up everything to the community: their person, their rights and their goods. However, it is important to note in what sense they give up their material possessions: interestingly, they do not actually hand over the right to exploit or appropriate them. Instead, they hand over something like the legal title to such possessions. As far as they are concerned, the sovereign power becomes 'master' of all their goods, but that does not mean that they lose the use or the benefit of such goods. In fact, Rousseau claims that such an arrangement makes the possession of them even more secure than they were before, since the individual has tied themselves into a network of mutual ownership which extends across the whole community. In a somewhat similar manner to our earlier discussion of freedom, the fact that everyone in the society is in the same boat means that each member actually has more assurance of being able to enjoy their property in peace, since for someone to violate their right to such property would entail a violation against the entire state.

So, somewhat confusingly perhaps, the state seems to have an important formal right over all the possessions of its constituents, and yet this does not, in Rousseau's view, diminish the real sense of them remaining the property of their (individual) owner. If we are to make sense of this, we need to follow his more general thoughts on the notion of property itself, and what kinds of action establish rights over it. As we might expect, Rousseau has no time for the view that one may establish property by the right of the strongest. Using the example of ownership of territory, he argues that if a person simply walks up to a piece of land and claims, by right of conquest, to 'own' it, then they are simply replicating the free-for-all of the state of nature. They may derive the material benefit of the land by such a manoeuvre, but they gain no surety over their claim, and if someone becomes strong enough to expel them from it then they will have no recourse to legal protection. This is what Rousseau means by his distinction between mere possessions, and property in its genuine sense. According to him, the actions of the Conquistadores and other explorers who dispossessed aboriginal peoples are just examples of this kind of activity, however much they may have been dressed-up with legal niceties after the event.

Nonetheless, Rousseau does acknowledge that a person may come into property via the right of the 'first occupant'. This is different to the right of the strongest in the following ways: first, the land (or goods) must not be inhabited (or used) by any prior occupants; second, the claimant should not take no more than that which they require for their reasonable subsistence; and third, the right of possession is actually established by making use of the property, and not letting it fall into idleness. In setting out these conditions, Rousseau is making use of a principle most famously articulated by the English philosopher John Locke.[7] Locke argued that all rights to property ultimately descend from the ownership we have, by default, of our own bodies. Any actions we subsequently take which involve the appropriation of goods in the furtherance of our own survival (collecting food, building shelter or cultivating land) may be construed as the reasonable accumulation of property. What fixes such things as *our* property is the fact that we have mixed the labour of our own bodies with them. This situation presents few problems in the pre-technological state, since there is a limit to the resources an individual or a family could possibly consume, and the scope for competing claims is small. But once agriculture and other technology extend the acquisitive powers of each individual, and people start to conglomerate in large groups, then the problem of overlapping or unequal title to property becomes serious. So it is that Rousseau's conditions on property ownership are necessary: an individual may only acquire that which they can make use of, and should not accumulate more than they need.

Such is the conception of property based on the 'first occupant' principle. Rousseau claims that this is understood even in the state of nature, though it may not always be strongly protected. This is because, in his view, in the absence of a first convention each individual is still acting more or less on their own. Though the bulk of the populace may recognize the validity of title granted by the first occupant principle, there is no absolute guarantee that they will. Indeed, it is likely that the human weaknesses of jealousy and resentment will sorely test the widely accepted principles of property rights. What is needed, according to Rousseau, is an extension of the weak notion of first occupancy into something firmer and more certain. The renunciation of every individual's rights over their property to the state is, paradoxically enough, his way of achieving such extra legal protection. His thinking is that in his ideal social order each member of the community will be regarded as a trustee of property ultimately owned by the state. As the basis for all ownership lies in the very foundation of the community as a whole, each person will respect the division of possessions as much as they respect the contractual basis of their social order. To put it more crudely, it will be harder for any one individual to violate the terms of a system held in common by all of their fellow citizens than it would be to violate another individual's rights in isolation.

For Rousseau, as with his conception of civil freedom, this situation has the effect of enhancing the legitimacy of property ownership. Instead of each individual's acquisitions being theirs by virtue of the relatively weak first occupant principle, they are now underwritten by the entire community. This may become slightly more obvious if we consider the picture, as Rousseau does, from the perspective of someone *outside* the community. Suppose a member of a rival state casts a greedy eye over a portion of land bordering their own. They may decide to seize it by force, and add it to their own dominion. If the individual who already owns the land does so purely on their own account, then the invader only has to overcome that one person's resistance to accomplish their goal. However, if the land in question is legally owned by the whole community of which the current owner is a member, then the invader will have to contend with the entire state if they wish to seize it. And this is one reason why Rousseau believes his system of property provides real benefits for parties to *The Social Contract*: as trustees of possessions held in common by a far more powerful force than they are, each derives far more security over what they own than they would have done otherwise. In addition, we may presume that the settlement of disputes *between* individuals within the state is also made more certain and less capricious, as any misdemeanour is committed against the entire state, not just a person on their own. Such inter-connectedness is a powerful reason for all to respect the position of the other, and the ground for Rousseau's claim that property rights are *more* secure under his system than otherwise.

Now, we may accept Rousseau's points about the added security of property held by the state against outside interference. However, as with our consideration of freedom, we may be worried by the power the state itself seems to have over every individual's right to property. What is to stop the sovereign deciding to appropriate property as it pleases? If the general will directs it to take, say, 10 per cent of everyone's possessions, what protection does the populace have? After all, in legal terms, everything they own actually belongs to the state in the first place. It may seem that Rousseau assumes, as earlier, that the state's actions will be uniformly benign.

Perhaps in order to meet this objection, he makes a quite complicated point about the precise nature of the state's ownership of all property. According to him, the state only ever owns the property of its members by the aforementioned principle of first occupant.

So the state itself, from its perspective, has no more title to the goods of all than does an individual over their possessions in the state of nature. By contrast, the individual citizen within Rousseau's state has a *greater* purchase on the possessions within their trusteeship, since, as he has argued, this is underwritten by the whole community acting in concert.

This is an odd point to make. Presumably, Rousseau is aiming to quell worries over the potential abuse of individual rights by the state – after all, in his account the right of occupancy is a weaker right than that established by *The Social Contract*, with important limitations placed on it. But despite this qualification, it is still clear that, in every important sense, the state genuinely owns the property held in trust by every member of the community. There is still no obvious reason why the sovereign power could not simply decide, in accordance with the general will, to disinherit its members, or simply take things from them whenever it wished.

This is an analogous objection to the one we raised earlier with respect to freedom. Rousseau has outlined a system which he claims brings great benefits, but which also places (apparently) enormous power in the hands of the sovereign, and seems to generate no safeguards against abuse of that power. If the individual lacks tools with which to ward off capricious or unjust behaviour, then there must be some other reason why the sovereign cannot simply ride roughshod over the interests of any one of its members. And, as intimated earlier, Rousseau feels he does have such reasons. These pertain to the unique nature of the general will: he will aim to demonstrate how this concept, properly understood, constrains the sovereign from acting partially or unjustly and ensures that each individual within the state will be free in the best possible sense. In order to see how this mechanism will work, we must now turn, at last, to his exposition of the workings of the sovereign in Book II.

SUMMARY

It may be helpful at this stage to have a brief recapitulation of the main themes we have covered.

Rousseau's aim is to devise a political system which preserves the freedom found in the state of nature while avoiding the material dangers of such a state. He considers a number of current political theories, each dependent on the idea of a certain group (or an individual) having power over a subordinate populace. He rejects these because, among other things, the relationships of dependence and patronage they encourage are inimical to true freedom. In these poorly constructed societies, argues Rousseau, humanity's natural inclinations of benign self-interest and compassion are replaced by an excessive self-regard, which in turn fosters despotism and inequality.

His alternative society is formed when all potential members decide to relinquish their individual freedoms in favour of a community of equals. Each person enters into a contract where their individual liberty is exchanged for a communal 'civil liberty'. Every member of the resultant state is in the same position, and no-one retains a greater or lesser degree of freedom or influence. The decisions of the state are made by the sovereign body, which is composed of all members of the state. These decisions reflect the general will of the community, and are binding on all.

The advantage of such a system, Rousseau claims, is that each citizen finds their moral understanding uplifted, and their freedom (properly understood) enhanced. By being compelled to participate in a genuinely cooperative endeavour, they are released from their bonds of narrow self-interest and take their place as citizens of a properly legitimate political order. However, he is yet to explain precisely how the actions of the sovereign achieve this transformation, or why his system will avoid the lapse into despotism which afflicts rival political theories.

STUDY QUESTIONS

1. What are the chief strengths and weaknesses of the three political systems Rousseau rejects, in his own account? Are his reasons for dismissing them valid ones?
2. How does humanity progress from the state of nature into the state of society, according to Rousseau? Is his description of the changes a compelling one?
3. What are the essential features of Rousseau's social model, as outlined in Book I? What are the potential benefits and pitfalls of such a system?
4. What are the principal differences between 'natural liberty' and 'civil liberty', as outlined by Rousseau? What are the advantages and disadvantages of each conception?

5.   What is Rousseau's conception of property within civil society? Is he right that property which is publicly owned is the most legitimate form of possession?

BOOK II

In Book II, Rousseau concentrates on making the nature of the sovereign clearer, and also expanding on the currently nebulous idea of the general will. By doing so, he hopes to show that the worries we have about the apparently unfettered powers of the sovereign can be met. He also has points to make about the practicalities of government, some of which will be discussed in more detail in Book III, and much to say about the law and its proper application. In doing so, he introduces the character of the lawgiver, a figure which has seemed to many commentators the most confusing aspect of his entire system. By the end of the book, however, he has advanced the bulk of the legislative basis of his political system, and we will be in a much better position to judge the success of it.

The nature of the sovereign (1–2)

Rousseau begins with two claims about the nature of the sovereign: that it is inalienable, and that it is indivisible. The first idea is something of a reiteration of an idea he has already raised in his discussion of slavery. As we saw then, he believes that a person cannot give away or sell their essential freedom to another individual or group. If such a thing were done, then the seller would lose an essential element of their proper humanity, and thus cease to be a meaningful party to the agreement. The only circumstance in which an individual can give up their freedom without incurring this penalty is if the transaction takes place as part of *The Social Contract* we have been exploring. As every other party to this contract also renders up their own liberty to an equal degree, Rousseau argues that all benefit from a greater and more profound 'civil liberty', and only give up their prior freedom in order to receive an improved version of it in return.

Reasonably enough, given his general position, Rousseau argues that once this exchange has been made there can be no further alienation of the sovereign body. In other words, after every individual has transferred their individual freedom to the sovereign, that power cannot be further delegated or given away to another group. To do so would break the essential feature of Rousseau's social order: that all members of the community participate to an equal level in the deliberations of the sovereign, and all are bound to an equal level by its decisions. If a group of members of the state decided that they were somehow more fitted to govern the community than others, and seized the role of determining the general will and acting on it (whether by force or the agreement of all others), then the social order would degenerate into the kind of stratified society which Rousseau is trying to avoid. In such a scenario, all the individual members of the state would have given up their freedoms, but only a subset of them would have retained the power to shape the direction of the community. And this, of course, is just another version of Grotius's scenario of a people choosing to give up their freedom to a monarch (or oligarchy), which Rousseau has already rejected.

It is important to note here that Rousseau is not claiming that no powers at all can be delegated from the sovereign downwards. On a practical level, it would be very difficult to run a society if everything had to be decided by an assembly of all its members. As we shall see, many of the practical decisions affecting the community are in fact taken by the government, which is a subordinate level of administration. The sole task of the sovereign is to determine the general will, and to act according to its dictates. However, once this claim has been made we are likely to want to know more from Rousseau about how such labour is divided up. What makes one issue a matter for the sovereign, and another a matter for government? In other words, which kinds of issues require attention to be paid to the general will, which ones can be left for subordinate administrative bodies to sort out?

Rousseau's answers to this give us more clues to the nature of the general will and how it must operate. He begins by claiming that the sovereign, as well as being inalienable, is also indivisible. This is a very similar idea to the one just considered, but this time refers directly to the issue of separation of powers, a discussion which Rousseau would have been familiar with from the writings of Locke.[8] In many political systems in both our own time and Rousseau's own, the sovereign power of a nation is divided into several elements. Most commonly, these are the executive (the body charged with implementing laws and policies), the legislature (which formulates the laws themselves) and the judiciary (which adjudicates on the correct application or transgression of such laws). In Rousseau's account, there is no such division of the sovereign power. The sovereign only has one job: to determine what the general will is, and pass regulations in accordance with its dictates. When this process is followed correctly, the regulations which emerge may properly be called 'laws'. If any subdivision of the state (i.e. the government, or an individual) passes its own regulations, then even though they may be in some sense binding, they are merely 'decrees'.

This conception of the role of the sovereign cuts across many more familiar schemes of national administration. For example, as Rousseau points out, the act of declaring war is commonly held to be a fundamental prerogative of the sovereign body of a nation. However, in his own political system, all the sovereign does is pass laws in accordance with demands of the general will. According to Rousseau, the decision to go to war is properly understood as the *implementation* of a law. So waging war is not a genuine function of the sovereign: if Rousseau's ideal community were to decide to do such a thing, then the decision would rest with some other administrative element of it. Of course, it is likely that the sovereign would have the job of passing laws to determine under what circumstances wars may be declared, or when they are forbidden, etc. The point is that the sovereign body has no role in acting upon those laws: that is a task which must be carried out by a different element of the society.

So we are beginning to get a clearer picture of the role and limits of sovereign power in Rousseau's scheme. First, it is necessary that every action of the sovereign is performed when it is functioning as a whole: there can be no delegation of this role to groups composed of less than all members of the community. Second, the sovereign is limited to passing laws, not enacting them. If either of these conditions is broken, then the actions of the sovereign (or elements therein) may no longer be considered legitimate. This is because, as we already know, the legitimacy of the sovereign body comes from the fact that it is fully representative, and also that its dictates apply to all members of the community. In due course, Rousseau has quite a lot to say about what happens when nations succumb to corruption of the proper function of sovereignty, but for now he is concerned to delineate the sovereign's function and its associated powers. And it should be clear that such moves are partly designed to address some of the worries about the apparently unfettered powers of the sovereign we raised earlier. As the sovereign power is in the business of simply making laws, not acting upon them, it is not within its remit to perform some kinds of malfeasance directly, such as arbitrarily seizing an individual's property. And since every law is passed in an assembly composed of all members of the state, there will be no cases (we are told) in which a particular interest group could pass a discriminatory law just on its own account. In Rousseau's phrase, the law applies to all because it comes from all, and that is the only basis of legitimacy.

However, even though these moves might help quell some objections over the extent of sovereign power, we are still left with some key questions. Despite the fact that the decisions of the sovereign body must be made by all of its members in concert, what is to stop a majority faction within it from dominating the proceedings? And even if the sovereign cannot *act* unjustly, what is to stop it passing unjust laws? Rousseau's answer to such questions lies, at least to start with, in an elucidation of the nature of the general will, and also the nature of laws. The latter notion is dealt with at length in the second half of Book II, but the former is addressed straightaway. As a precursor to that discussion, Rousseau reiterates some features of the general will which have already been indicated.

First, he claims that there is no great regularity of coincidence between the general will and the particular will of each individual. There is no great surprise here: this is simply the claim that most people, most of the time, will have a pretty good idea of what they themselves want in the short term. However, the individual may not see clearly the benefit of pursuing a course of action in which the whole community benefits, even if, in the long term, they themselves would end up being better off than they would have been by acting selfishly. Or they may be quite aware of which course of action would benefit everyone, themselves included, but yet opt to take the choice which yields immediate results for them. Rousseau claims that there can never be a guarantee that the individual will of each member of the society will reliably run alongside their general will, since the former inherently tends towards partiality, while the latter is exclusively concerned with equality. However, each of us does have the potential, at least within a properly regulated society, to act in accordance with our general will (i.e. to pursue the course which will benefit all equally). Here the notion is portrayed just as we defined it in the previous chapter: the motivation we all have as individuals to do what is in the interests of the community as a whole.

Second, the general will is the only reliable guide to the successful and fair administration of a community. If properly discerned and acted upon, it holds the promise of charting a path for the state which protects both freedom and security. Any decision made by the sovereign which has as its object a part of the community, rather than the whole of it, cannot have emerged from a proper application of the general will. And here the notion of the general will seems to be referred to by Rousseau in a slightly different way. Rather than being the term for a motivation we all have individually, it seems to be the standard or guide against which the sovereign assesses its options. When conceived thus, Rousseau seems to regard the general will as something uniquely possessed by the people acting together, a concept which is only actualized through the activities of the sovereign itself. As he puts it,

> either the will is general or it is not; either it is the will of the people, or merely that of a part. (*SC*, II, 2)

This is a little confusing. It seems that the general will is at once a motivation present in each one of us, and also a property of the community as a whole. Indeed, throughout *The Social Contract*, Rousseau seems to oscillate between these two senses more or less without compunction. For this reason among others, the very notion of the general will has remained an object of much controversy among those trying to make sense of Rousseau's thought. However, it should be obvious that unless we can glean some more concrete information about how this elusive idea works in the greater political scheme, we will be unable properly to assess Rousseau's enterprise as a whole. So, as the following two chapters contain some of his most extensive comments on the general will in the entire book, it is time to grasp the nettle and see if we can reconstruct a clear account of what, precisely, it is.

The nature of the general will (3–4)

The apparent confusion between the general will as possessed by individuals and the general will as exercised by the sovereign points to the central difficulty Rousseau faces. He wants to argue that individuals in his just society remain as free as they were before giving up their rights in *The Social Contract*. So it is important that when the sovereign passes a law, it in some way reflects *their* aspirations and desires. If it didn't in some sense do this, then it is difficult to see how it is *their* freedom which is enhanced and protected. On the other hand, the very attraction of the general will is that it is decoupled from individual drives and partial desires, and reflects a somewhat impersonal set of objectives for the community as a whole. How can Rousseau present a picture of the general will which respects its aspect as a reflection of individual motivations and also its role as the guiding principle of the whole society?

Perhaps the most obvious move he could make here would be to insist that the general will is simply the unanimous decision of the entire society. We already know that the sovereign body is composed of every adult in the community. If such an assembly were to deliberate on a particular issue, and if all were agreed on a particular course of action with respect to that issue, would that not be an example of the will of the sovereign being properly 'general'? In such a case, each member would have exercised their own motivation to act for the good of the community through the procedure of voting, so the former sense of the general will as something possessed by every member is recognized. And the sovereign can also genuinely be said to have expressed the will of the people as a whole, since there have been no dissensions. Moreover, since the entire community has opted to pursue a single course, it is more likely than not that the policy is a good one – if it were not, there would surely be at least some dissension from it. As long as the decision is of the proper sort (the passing of a law, rather than a resolution to act in a certain way), and there has been no clandestine coercion or deception, is this not a clear picture of what the general will must be?

Well, not quite. We can already see practical objections mounting. Even though a unanimous decision may give the assembly some confidence that their resolution is correct, this guarantee is still very weak. Rousseau has previously intimated that the general will is a very reliable (or even infallible) guide to what laws the society should pass. It is very easy to imagine a case where, for lack of information, cultural mores or simply stupidity, a unanimous decision turns out to be bad, repressive or discriminatory. In addition, we may wonder how likely it is that a community will ever agree on all matters of import with total unanimity. As Rousseau is aware, one of the core problems of political association is balancing the conflicting desires and wills of the state's members fairly. As he has already observed, particular wills are forever pulling in different, partial directions. Given this is so, the condition of unanimity would risk condemning the sovereign to impotence. For these reasons, he rejects the idea that the general will is best understood as a unanimous vote by the sovereign body. Indeed, he explicitly contrasts the 'will of all' with the general will, claiming that although the entire populace can never be corrupted, they can be misled or work from faulty information.

If a unanimous verdict is too ambitious a standard for the sovereign to work to in every case, then perhaps a simple majority of the voting members is enough. In a footnote at the beginning of Chapter 2, Rousseau seems to indicate that this is an acceptable basis for determining the general will, and explains that unanimity is not required for a decision to reflect the general will as long as all votes are counted and no-one is excluded from contributing to the process (*SC*, II, 2n). But we must be careful here. Rousseau still wants to claim that the general will is in some way a reflection of the will of the community as a whole. As we shall see shortly, the kind of majority voting system based on competing parties which we are familiar with in our own democratic societies is not a suitable model. He is instead keen to preserve the idea that the 'will of all' forms the basis of the general will, even if the two notions are not quite the same thing. In a rather baffling passage, he attempts to clarify the relationship between the two notions thus:

> There is often a great difference between the will of all [what all individuals want] and the general will; the general will studies only the common interest while the will of all studies private interest, and it is indeed no more than the sum of individual desires. But if we take away from these same wills the pluses and minuses which cancel each other out, the balance which remains is the general will. (*SC*, II, 3)

Here is a concrete-looking statement of what the general will is. It is derived from the will of all through a mechanical process of addition and subtraction. If this process could be made clear, then we would be able to see precisely how the general will is generated. Unfortunately, Rousseau fails to say much more about it, so if we are to understand his thought here we must do some work on his behalf.

The language of arithmetic used by Rousseau is perhaps not very helpful. A bit more light is shed by the accompanying footnote to the quoted passage, where he talks of the 'opposition' between different wills yielding a harmonious result. We might begin to try and make sense of this as follows. Citizen A wishes to propose a law for the community which will result in some benefit to himself and his family. He takes it to the sovereign assembly, where the proposal is debated. Although the sovereign body agrees that Citizen A will improve his situation should the law be enacted (which all else being equal is a good thing), it also turns out that a second member, Citizen B, stands to lose from the situation. As a result, her particular will leads her to oppose the resolution. The two particular wills, that of Citizens A and B cancel each other out (which is analogous to Rousseau's talk of 'pluses and minuses'). As the 'sum' of these competing wills is zero, then the sovereign may well conclude that the proposal does not reflect the genuine general will of the entire community, and reject the proposal.

However, suppose that Citizens C, D and E also stand to benefit from the original proposal, and that they comprise the rest of this (very small) community. In such a situation, only Citizen B loses out, and everyone else does well. It may then look to the sovereign body as if the proposal does reflect a course of action of benefit to the entire community, even though one element of it suffers. To use the analogy of the body once again, it may be like a runner accepting that their knees will get a bit of wear and tear as the price for ensuring that their body as a whole stays fit and healthy. Similarly, Citizen B's wellbeing may be curtailed somewhat, but everyone else does well, so the proposal reflects what could legitimately be described as the general will of the community as a whole. Citizen B's particular will is out of sync with that of everyone else, so even if she 'cancels out' the will of Citizen A, the fact that C, D and E all support him means that the 'balance' indicates his proposal is in concordance with the general will.

How convincing is this as a reconstruction of Rousseau's views? In the very crude form outlined here, it is surely inadequate. For Citizen B in particular, it must seem as if she has just been ganged-up on by a majority who wish to benefit at her expense. She is in a minority to be sure, but that in itself cannot be the only factor which relegates her interests from the calculation. After all, in the state of nature there is nothing to stop larger groups of people with a temporary common interest from picking on smaller ones, and this is precisely the kind of inequality which Rousseau is opposed to. What is missing seems to be a consideration on the part of each member of the sovereign about what consequences their actions will have on the health of the *entire* community. If they were to pass the law discriminating against Citizen B, then they would have established a precedent that the majority interest is by itself sufficient grounds to approve legislation. And this means that should circumstances change none of them will be safe in future from the same thing happening to them. It may seem to them then, if they are inclined to think the issue through, that the security they gained from being a party to *The Social Contract* has just disappeared, and that the actions of the sovereign are simply the instrument of whichever group of people, with whatever temporary or contingent interests, happens to be acting in concert at any given time.

So the calculus whereby the general will is derived from the will of all must be more nuanced than a process which simply disregards those views which are out of kilter with the majority. And although we still have work to do to see how it might be suitably modified to take account of this objection, Rousseau does make two further claims about the operation of the general which move us towards a possible solution.

First, he explicitly rules out the legitimacy of factionalism or partisanship within the sovereign body. The existence of interest groups is to be strictly banned. His reasons are as follows. We know that the legitimate general will is derived from the will of all the members of the sovereign body, and that the process involves something of an 'averaging' or 'refining' of those initial disparate wills. Given that this is so, it will be better if the sovereign body is able to consider the largest range of individual wills on any given subject. The more points of view the assembly is able to consider, the more likely it is that the spread will reflect an underlying trend or 'mean' view. We might think of how opinion polls work for an illustration of this. If I only interview five people out of a population of millions to discover the nation's voting intentions at the next general election, I am very likely to get an inaccurate result. The more raw data I can acquire in the form of individual intentions, the more confident I will be that the results of the poll correspond closely to the intention of the nation as a whole. In a somewhat analogous way, Rousseau claims that the more 'raw' unadulterated wills are expressed in the sovereign assembly, the greater chance there is that the process of refining will deliver a good approximation of the legitimate general will. If factions (political parties, interest groups, unions, etc.) are allowed to influence the debate on a given law, then the number of possible voices diminishes to the number of active factions plus any unaligned independents. In the worst case, one group becomes so powerful that it dominates all such discussions, and the sovereign degenerates into the mouthpiece for a subset of the community.

Rousseau proposes therefore that individual members of the sovereign be barred from communicating with each other during their deliberations. It is hard to believe that this is meant entirely literally – it would surely be impossible to stop people for talking among themselves prior to or during a debate on the adoption of an important law. In such a case, the operations of the sovereign would grind to a halt. However, there are some practical measures which could be taken which would limit the power of factions and parties. First, the ballot could be secret, which would curtail the ability of putative party leaders to control their members. Second, there could be strict rules decided on by the sovereign banning formal associations within the ambit of its work. Third, there could be practical measures put in place during the deliberations themselves, such as a guarantee of equal time for each member to speak. Whether or not it would ever be possible to prevent factions from asserting themselves at all, it does seem reasonable to suppose that their influence could be minimized through measures such as these. The more successful these measures are, Rousseau argues, the greater the likelihood that the will of all will provide a sound basis for ascertaining the general will.

So we can imagine a situation where Citizens A, C, D and E are prevented from formally acting in concert with one another in order to frustrate Citizen B. Even though all of them stand to benefit from Citizen A's proposed change in the law, they could not openly form an association within the sovereign body to lobby for it. Nonetheless, even if effective restrictions were placed on their overt cooperation, there would still be nothing to stop them, during a session of the sovereign body, from independently reaching the conclusion that the law change would advantage them, and combining their individual wills to stymie the objections of Citizen B. And if this is done merely to satisfy some material or prudential desire of theirs, then it looks like a pretty poor description of a 'general' will. Accordingly, Rousseau makes a further important point about the kinds of laws the sovereign can legitimately pass, which qualifies its actions a little more:

> The general will, to be truly what it is, must be general in its purpose as well as in its nature; that it should spring from all for it

to apply to all; and that it loses its natural rectitude when it is directed towards any particular and circumscribed object. (*SC*, II, 4)

So the general will, as well as deriving from the community as a whole, can only result in laws which apply to the community as a whole. Indeed, Rousseau explicitly states that a decision of the general will cannot be relied upon to adjudicate in a dispute between individuals or factions, or to pinpoint issues of concerns which are by their nature only of interest to a subset of the entire state (again, in *SC*, II, 4).

The effect of this condition is to limit the sorts of laws a sovereign body can pass quite dramatically. It could not, for example, pass a law where the explicit object was to deprive Citizen B of her property. In such a case, the will behind the law would be partial, even if the vast majority of the sovereign body voted for it. As Rousseau says, in this situation the disadvantaged party would feel themselves to have been subject to a partial will, and the terms of *The Social Contract* – the basis of the social order – would have been broken. The bargain she has struck in surrendering her liberty to all has been rendered void, since she is being governed by a partial, rather than a properly general, will, and can therefore quite properly claim she is not getting what she was promised in return.

So, within this condition in mind, what sorts of things count as legitimate areas for the sovereign to pronounce upon? Rousseau does not give us an exhaustive list of suitably general topics. This is not surprising, since the important feature of the law is its formal aspect: that it comes from all and applies to all. The content of the law is less important to Rousseau, with the proviso that the general will which determines it must be of such a sort that the ultimate good for the community is its object. However, it does seem to be the case that Rousseau has in mind laws of a fundamental nature, ones which are limited to regulating the more basic principles of social organization. He refers to such political, or fundamental, laws later on (*SC*, II, 12), and makes clear that these are the subject of his enquiry. To see why this is, we might recall the reasons why individuals enter into social arrangements in the first place. The state of nature presents clear threats to basic security, to the preservation of the property individuals need in order to survive and to their ability peacefully to enjoy the fruits of their labours. It is primarily in order to preserve these things that people decide to come together in a society, and therefore it is most obviously over these things that the sovereign of a properly constituted social order will be competent to dictate terms. The important feature of these basic needs is that everyone has a more or less equal desire towards them. We all need to have such requirements met, and if any society failed to guarantee them then we would have no cause to remain part of it. We could never have a reason to assent to a social order which failed to guarantee these fundamental goods, since we may as well take our chances back in the state of nature. By the same token, we will always have a reason to assent to a law which protects and preserves these fundamental goods.

Understood thus, the actions of the sovereign may in practice be limited to a relatively small set of issues, albeit of considerable importance. We could characterize these issues as the fundamental principles of society: laws which regulate the provision of the most basic needs and social goods. Though there is of course no external guarantee that the sovereign will restrict itself to such areas, understood thus the sovereign may seem somewhat less sinister and all-powerful with regard to the lives of its constituent citizens. A sovereign body working properly under such conditions would have no business picking out individuals or groups within the society for special treatment. If the sovereign resolved, for example, to confiscate the property of a particular citizen who was disliked or awkward, then it would not be acting in a suitably general way, and so could not possibly be pursuing the general will. If such actions on the part of the sovereign were tolerated or defended by the state as a whole, then the community could no longer be described as operating under Rousseau's principles for a justly ordered society.

To return to our speculative example of Citizen A's proposed law change, if his draft legislation were to be of the required sort, it would have to be such that it neither picked out Citizen A's nor Citizen B's interests explicitly, but was designed to provide a general rule for the whole community to follow. Moreover, the objective of such a rule would have to be the safeguarding or enhancement, again for the entire community, of the fundamental principles of the social order. If the sovereign were to act in such a manner, and the law were to be appropriately drafted, then Citizen B could have no complaint with the ruling. As mentioned earlier, if she continued to protest under such conditions, then she would be forced to comply with the ruling by her fellow citizens: there can be no ducking out of laws passed by the sovereign simply because they don't suit an individual or partial interest. The reason that such coercion is justified is that Citizen B, according to this account, actually has good reason to accept the ruling, since its object is solely to preserve the fundamental principles of the state of which she is a part.

In the final few paragraphs of Chapter 4 of Book II, Rousseau extols the virtues of a social order run along these lines. Because the sovereign body is constituted and operates according to principles all have voluntarily assented to, its dictates are uniquely legitimate. And since it cannot by its nature impose its power 'beyond the limits of the general covenants', which we may take to mean the general under-standing on the part of the citizens that the laws will apply to all equally, it will not act capriciously or malevolently. Although no individual retains any rights to resist the dictates of the sovereign, this renunciation does not amount to a significant loss of genuine freedom, since what is being thrown away is the right to an uncertain and violent life, and what is being offered in return is a stable, secure environment where the interests of all are protected by an assembly of all. As we have seen, the price of surrendering all individual free-dom to the sovereign body, such that each member may be 'forced to the free' when necessary, is essential if the universal character of the social order is to be maintained.

Discerning the general will (Book IV, 1–2)

Despite these conditions placed on the operation of the sovereign, we might still feel somewhat uneasy about Rousseau's claim that dissent-ing voices should be forced to comply with the general will by the rest of the citizens. And yet there is no doubt that Rousseau feels such a strong line is always justified, so long as the sovereign is properly instituted and the laws produced by it are suitably general in nature. In the first two chapters of Book IV, Rousseau says much of interest concerning the nature of the general will and how it is to be deter-mined and acted upon by the sovereign. His treatment of the issues there directly addresses the worry that such coercion defeats the requirement that each individual within the state of *The Social Con-tract* remains as free as they were before entering it. Given the relative detail of his response there, we shall take a brief detour through these passages before returning to the point we have reached in Book II.

Rousseau frames the question thus: 'How can an opposing minority be both free and subject to laws to which they have not consented?' (*SC*, IV, 2). Part of the answer has already been given: if the sovereign has been acting properly, then it can never will anything which the individual does not have sufficient reason to assent to, and thus their opposition is based either on a misunderstanding, or malice or on a misplaced desire to assert a particular will over that of the entire community.

In an illuminating passage, Rousseau gives us some indication of how this works by outlining the proper considerations for each voting member of the sovereign. When a proposal comes up in a session of the sovereign body, each individual member is to weigh up not whether they approve or disapprove of a particular proposition, but rather whether they think that such a proposition is in concordance with their understanding of the general will. After the discussion has concluded, the casting of votes itself directly 'yields a declaration of the general will' (*SC*, IV, 2). This is the final verdict on the matter, such that any dissenters should then conclude that they have simply made a mistake over a matter of fact: they thought they were reflecting the general will by opposing the proposition, whereas the general will, properly understood, dictated that the proposition be adopted. Their proof of this is simply that the majority has ruled thus. The good citizen will, in such a case, acknowledge their mistake and be thankful that the sovereign has ruled otherwise. Should they fail to do so, the state is justified in forcing them to comply.

For this state of affairs to be persuasive, it must be the case that the sovereign is an extremely reliable instrument, both in terms of discerning what the general will is, and in acting in accordance with it. If this is not how things are, then we must doubt whether the individual has good reason to surrender all their rights to such a body. But what happens if the sovereign assembly, honestly and after applying due diligence, simply fails to diagnose what the best course for the community is? The citizens may endeavour to pick out the general will correctly, and might well think they have adopted the right policy, but actually opt for a law which has disastrous and iniquitous effects. This would seem to be a perfectly plausible scenario, and yet Rousseau has considerable confidence that under the conditions he outlines the correct course of action for the community will in fact be readily apparent. In the first two chapters of Book IV, he adds a series of comments on the general will which make this optimism clear:

> So long as several men assembled together consider themselves a single body, they have only one will, which is directed towards their common preservation and general well-being. Then all the animating forces of the state are vigorous and simple [. . .]; the common good makes itself so manifestly evident that only common sense is needed to discern it. (*SC*, IV, 1)

Why does Rousseau think that matters are so clear-cut, and the possibility of error so distant? As we will see, this comment is somewhat at variance with claims he makes in Book II, which we will consider below, about the need for the guiding hand of a benign lawgiver. But in advance of that, there are some reasons for his optimism that the properly constituted sovereign assembly will tend to find the dictates of the general will evident and obvious.

The first is his familiar insistence on the natural goodness of people in their unadulterated, pre-civilized state. To recall, for Rousseau, it is primarily the actions of poorly constituted societies which alienate people from their healthy instincts towards self-preservation and compassion. In the absence of the distorting drives of malign *amour-propre*, people will generally perceive what is good and healthy for them, free from the distractions of the need to maintain a social station. Under the conditions of *The Social Contract*, they are free to maintain this benign and uncluttered disposition within a properly ordered society, and so retain their clear view of the right course of action to take in order to preserve the social good. As Rousseau is fond of claiming, each individual in their role as a citizen member of the sovereign has become a constituent part of a single willing entity. Just as each individual in their role as a discrete entity has a clear vision of what is needed for their own body, so the sovereign has a clear vision of what is needed to sustain and guide the state. Rousseau further claims that the simplest intellects are best at retaining this natural instinct for the best route to successful self-preservation. 'Upright and simple men' are the most difficult to deceive or trick because they have insufficient complexity in their wants and needs to be capable of subversion. The society of *The Social Contract* respects this simple, direct goodness, and through the agency of such ideal citizens acting within the sovereign body correctly discerns the general will of the entire community.

It is not hard to feel that Rousseau is once more being rather too optimistic here about the natural goodness of human beings and their innate ability to know what is good for the community as a whole. Aside from the psychological considerations we discussed at the start of this book, most of which were stated as matters of fact rather than argued for, why should we agree with him that simple, uneducated folk are the best judges of the common good, and that more sophisticated types are more liable to be led astray? Rousseau does not provide much in the way of detailed evidence to support his views, but instead argues that the reason we may find such a suggestion intuitively absurd is that we are used to living in poorly constituted societies where the qualities of simplicity, directness and honesty are not valued. Our perception of the proper general will is dim because we have been encouraged for so long to champion and pursue our own individual desires and projects. In support of this notion that simple, representative societies are better at resisting corruption of the general will, Rousseau claims that the political entities of his own time closest to the ideal state he advocates, Geneva and Berne, would never have tolerated a tyrant such as Cromwell: the very sophistication of such dens of iniquity as London or Paris is what enables the silver-tongued rogue to seize control of the reins of power and for the common good to be lost sight of.

This argument may seem rather weak in itself, but does point to a more general consideration which Rousseau trades on. He consistently wants to claim that society, rather than nature, shapes the moral character of individuals. In badly-run societies, individuals will tend towards destructive modes of behaviour; in properly-run ones, they will be able to flourish. The reason why we perhaps find the idea of a cooperative body of like-minded individuals successfully and simply discerning and acting upon a general will hard to credit is because, living as we do in a poorly constituted political order, we have never witnessed such a thing ourselves. Given the right social framework, and the psychology which Rousseau says we possess, it would at least be likely that the moral characters of citizens would improve to the point where their motivation to act in accordance with the general will is much stronger than ours. The proof of the pudding, we are asked to believe, is in the eating.

The plausibility of this scheme depends at least partly on the plausibility of Rousseau's earlier claims about human nature and our inherent knowledge of what is good for us, since the reliability of the sovereign's deliberations depends on this. If we find this idea dubious, we are not likely to find the political system as a whole convincing either. However, even if we are minded to concede to Rousseau that simple, unadulterated human nature will tend to point the sovereign body in the right direction with regard to the general will, there is still some qualification to be made. Even at his most optimistic, Rousseau never claims that the citizens of the ideal state are absolutely infallible in their discernment of the general will, so there does need to be some winnowing mechanism to knock out the rough edges of the sovereign's deliberations. We have already rejected the notion that unanimity must always be present for a decision to reflect the general will. According to Rousseau, the only act which always requires complete assent is the original agreement to participate in *The Social Contract* – once this undertaking has been entered into, it is sufficient for the purposes of determining laws that a majority obtains within the assembly. However, Rousseau does believe that the closer the vote is towards unanimity, assuming the conditions we outlined above have been met, the more closely the decision of the sovereign will correspond to the general will. In addition, the more important or difficult an issue is, the greater the majority will be needed before the sovereign will have confidence that the decision is in line with the general will. Finally, as we shall see below, Rousseau by no means thinks that every society formed according to his guidelines will be equally successful in generating a reliable vision of the general will, and where the fabric of the society is such as to render the sovereign's powers of perception relatively weak then the majority should be correspondingly larger again.

The presence of these 'error-diffusing' tactics indicates that, for Rousseau, the process of working out what the general will dictates is an imperfect one, even if it is generally good enough to warrant the enforced agreement of every citizen. In fact, at times it seems as though he himself oscillates between a very confident belief that a properly constituted society will virtually always be able to pick out the general will, and a somewhat resigned pessimism that the corruptibility of human nature will make such perception a rare and unusual thing.[9] Given the weakness of the arguments so far for the sovereign's reliability, we are perhaps likely to sympathize with the latter argument rather than the former. More is needed, we might think, to show how the sovereign reliably discerns the common good for all before we are wont to take Rousseau's word for it. Indeed, in his pessimistic moments he does advance two more considerations to try and shore this aspect of his theory up. The first is a requirement that the state be of such a kind that its constituents will readily see themselves as part of a shared enterprise. This is a matter of culture and demographics, and not all nations are as capable of achieving the necessary homogeneity or communal spirit. Second, the fallibility of the sovereign body also requires a guiding hand in order to prod it in the right direction. This is the enigmatic figure of the lawgiver, which has puzzled many readers of Rousseau and which remains highly contentious. We will look at both proposals in due course.

In advance of this, though, we need to consider one more worry about Rousseau's description of the sovereign so far. Let us accept for the time being that the sovereign in a properly constituted community *can* pick out the dictates of the general will reliably. What then is to prevent the members of that body from simply refusing to legislate in accordance with it? Even though they may see clearly what the correct course of action is for the entire community, and recognize that all will benefit in the long run if it is pursued, what sanction exists to prevent selfish members from voting to promote their own partial interests? The answer is: there is no such sanction. There is no watchdog for the sovereign body, or set of reserved rights which each individual possesses in case the general will is not respected. However, Rousseau does claim that any sovereign power which deliberately ignores the general will would cease to have any legitimacy, and the society would revert to a version of those poorly constructed political models which have already been rejected.

His thinking on this might run as follows: there is a way in which individuals can form an equitable political association. To do this, they must give up their individual freedoms to the community as a whole, in which the laws are promulgated by a sovereign assembly of all members. By its very nature and constitution, the sovereign has no function other than to regulate the fundamental principles of association which each member has freely opted to place in common. For as long as it does this, each citizen will be the recipient of a healthy and benign civil liberty, and will remain genuinely free while enjoying the security offered by the state. But if the sovereign systematically fails to respect the general will, then this civil freedom will disappear, and the social order will in effect cease to be that governed by *The Social Contract*, and will degenerate into a version of the rule of the strongest. There could never be a separate body charged with preventing this happening, since the sovereign is the supreme author of the state's laws. Moreover, there is only so much one could do to prevent people, having been shown a better way of living, opting to reject it all and return to a partial, grasping alternative. As long as a majority within the sovereign has sufficient sense of community and respect for the general will to vote down those who wish to place their individual aims ahead of it, the society will preserve itself.

So, according to Rousseau, the sovereign is a self-regulating entity. There is no external body overseeing its activities: either it acts properly, and the society will prosper, or it doesn't, and the experiment of *The Social Contract* has failed. As he remarks at the end of his passage on voting in Book IV:

> This [system of suffrage] presupposes, it is true, that all the characteristics of the general will are still to be found in the majority; when these cease to be there, no matter what position men adopt, there is no longer any freedom. (*SC*, IV, 2)

This regretful statement of the situation seems more than a little inadequate. An individual, when weighing up whether or not to become a party to Rousseau's social contract, might reasonably feel nervous that there is no recourse to any kind of exterior court of appeal should the sovereign body degenerate into a repressive or unjust instrument of power. Given that they retain no rights to rebel or even dissent, they would likely want reassurance that the sovereign is much more likely that not to retain its upright preoccupation with the common good, otherwise the risk they run in giving up all their natural freedom to such a body looks rash. And Rousseau, at least in his more pessimistic moments, seems to share this concern. As we noted above, he makes a couple of moves in order to make this bargain seem more reasonable, the first of which is to introduce the character of the lawgiver, a discussion of which we now turn to.

The law (5–6)

After our detour into Book IV, we now jump back to where we left off in Book II. After setting limits on the nature of the sovereign power, and making clear its role as a legislative body, Rousseau turns his attention to the nature of law itself. Unhelpfully for the reader seeking reassurance that the state really is a benign institution, his first argument is for the right of the community to impose the death penalty on those who defy its laws. In the provocatively cold terms into which he is liable to slip from time to time, Rousseau announces the situation thus:

> If a prince says to [a citizen]: 'It is expedient for the state that you should die', then he should die, because [. . .] his life is no longer the bounty of nature but a gift he has received conditionally from the state. (*SC*, II, 5)

At this point, the liberal critic may be liable to throw their hands up and despair. Isn't the very purpose of the state to preserve life? If the individual surrenders their liberty to a body which can take it away seemingly with impunity, in what sense could they be considered as free as they were before entering into *The Social Contract*?

Rousseau at least seems to acknowledge that his position requires more than the cursory justification he is sometime inclined to give his contentious points. He starts by addressing the counter-argument that a person cannot relinquish to the state that which they have no right to in the first place. It was commonplace in Rousseau's time to hold that a person had no right to take their own life, since this was a gift from God. So if an individual has no powers to take their own life, how could they transfer such a power to the state to enact? This point may have less force now than it did in the time Rousseau was writing, since it seems less obvious to many in the modern world that a person does not have the *right* to take their own life, even if such an act is generally to be deplored and counselled against. But Rousseau meets the objection not by imputing a natural right to suicide to the individual (which could in theory be transferred to the state), but by claiming that the risk of death is one which is rational for an individual to take on when passing from the state of nature into the civil state. Suppose I wish to eliminate the possibility that my life will be endangered by murderers (who may be roaming freely in the perilous state of nature). On that basis, I enter civil society on the promise that it will be free of murderers. If I were then to become one myself I could have no complaint when my own life becomes forfeit as a result. When becoming a party to *The Social Contract* I take on the risk that I may become a victim of the stringent rules which attracted me to it in the first place. But because the risk of death is much lower in civil society than it is in nature, it is still a gamble worth taking.

Now Rousseau is surely right to say that an individual wishing to derive the benefits of a society should abide by the rules of that society, even if the penalties for transgression may in principle be turned on them. But it doesn't necessarily follow that capital punishment is an outcome which it would be always rational to accept as a risk. If it were the case that the *only way* to rid a society of murderers were to execute all such killers when they are discovered, then Rousseau's argument may have some force. But if a society were capable of generally safeguarding against murder without recourse to capital punishment, then taking on the risk of being killed by the state is unreasonable. Since I have not transferred the right to take my own life explicitly to the state in the terms of *The Social Contract* (according to Rousseau), the rightness of capital punishment becomes a pragmatic question: if it is necessary for the maintenance of the state's beneficial protective powers that it has the right to kill its citizens, then it is a rational choice for the citizen to accept the risk of state-sanctioned execution in exchange for such protection. But this is assumed, rather than argued-for, in the text. We might be very sceptical that the state needs the power to execute its citizens in order to maintain the security of the populace as a whole, at least without being given more reason for this claim.

Rousseau's second argument in favour of the death penalty is somewhat different. If an individual violates a law which the sovereign has formulated then they are to be understood as breaking the terms of *The Social Contract*. As such, they have placed themselves outside the limits of the state, and should be treated by it as a foreign entity. Depending on the severity of the crime committed, Rousseau recommends that they either be deported or executed. Later in the same chapter his tone seems to soften a little, and he claims that frequent use of such powers by the state indicates weakness or laxity, and that no person should be put to death if there is a less severe way of dealing with the problem of their opposition to the sovereign's pronouncements. Nonetheless, he leaves the reader in no doubt that the power of the state over an individual is complete, even to the extent that it may legitimately take their lives.

Rousseau's insistence on this point is rather puzzling. Up until now, we have been considering the powers of the sovereign. As we have seen, this body is charged with passing laws of a general nature which govern the basic direction and principles of the state. Given that the actual enacting of the death penalty is incompatible with this (in that it singles out a single individual or group for punishment), it cannot fall to the sovereign to carry out this burden. Indeed, Rousseau claims that the sovereign body cannot itself execute an instance of capital punishment: instead, that function must fall to a subordinate level of government. As yet, we know very little of the other organs of power aside from the sovereign, and so the reason for his insertion of this issue here is a little unclear. Moreover, the question of capital punishment seems somewhat redundant in the wider explanatory scheme. On the face of it, everything Rousseau has said thus far would be just as compatible with a society which abjured state-sanctioned killing. As such, we may feel that Rousseau's arguments here are ill-founded, and do nothing to advance the acceptability of his general scheme. If anything, they are likely to undermine the plausibility of his overall project for little reward, and so we should not regard them as being in any way essential to the wider scheme.

In the following chapter, thankfully, Rousseau moves on to more familiar ground. Having once again explained the social pact and the social order it gives rise to, he proposes to say a little more about the kinds of laws it must pass in order to preserve itself. He starts by considering the idea of 'natural law'. This is the idea that there is justice inherent in things, which by the application of reason or knowledge of God's will we are capable of perceiving. According to such a legal tradition, a law may be considered more or less just depending on how closely it conforms to the underlying natural order from which it derives its power. Rousseau does not dispute the first part of this, and is happy to accept that a divine creator is the source of all natural law, and that the activities of reason are in principle capable of enabling people to act in accordance with it. Nonetheless, true to form, he does not believe that the great mass of people will follow such dictates with any regularity. If they did, then the state of nature would no doubt remain a benign place and the necessity for civil society would be obviated. There would be in fact no advantage to an individual in following a lawful path within the state of nature, since those around them who do not will gain considerable power at their expense.

The great advantage civil society brings to this situation is that all the people who are subject to the laws are themselves the authors of them. By participating in the process of sovereignty, each member of the community is involved in making the law; and as a part of the state, each member is also subject to it. Because all have freely contracted themselves into civil society, and all participate in it, all are legitimately bound by the legal framework which emerges from the sovereign's actions. And, as we know already, for these laws properly to reflect the general will, they must apply to the entire state, and not pick out individuals or particular groups within it. In a rather complicated paragraph, Rousseau elaborates the problem with partial laws which have a definite object other than the community as a whole. A particular object of a law is either something outside the boundaries of the state, or something within them. If that object is an entity outside the state (say, a foreign power), then the general will has nothing to say about it, since the general will only comes from all and applies to all, and it cannot come from elements which play no part in the life of the community. On the other hand, if the object is within the state (say, a particular group of citizens with a common feature, such as teachers or artisans), then the state will be divided among itself, and the general will could once again not properly derive from all and apply to all.

However, it is not the case that laws need always have equal ramifications for every citizen in the state. Rousseau is not claiming that certain individuals or groups may never lose or benefit as a result of a law being passed: such a thing would be absurd. Indeed, he allows that the effect of laws may be to lay down certain privileges, or even to establish certain classes of society and the attributes needed to enter such classes. What a law could not do is specify which individual or group, simply by virtue of who they are, is to be treated in such and such a way. So a law could properly be passed which applied to all members of the community but which nonetheless had the effect of elevating the status of artisans and teachers, while a law which explicitly aimed to elevate the status of artisans or teachers and only applied to them could not be.

We have already raised some worries about the potential for injustice even in these kinds of laws. Rousseau is fond of using the analogy of the body to argue that the properly constituted sovereign could never pass a law which needlessly damaged any of the state's citizens. He claims that none of us as individuals could desire harm to come to our bodies, and since the political association created by *The Social Contract* binds all the constituents of the state into a single willing entity, the resultant political body is subject to the same aversion.

But even he seems to think, from time to time at least, that this analogy does not quite guarantee things will reliably work out for the best. In a remarkable passage, Rousseau voices some of the very objections we have raised earlier in our discussion on the discernment of the general will, and seems to concede that they are entirely valid:

> How can a blind multitude, which often does not know what it wants, because it seldom knows what is good for it, undertake by itself an enterprise as vast and difficult as a system of legislation? [. . .] The general will is always rightful, but the judgement which guides it not always enlightened. [. . .] Individuals see the good and reject it; the public desires the good and does not see it. (*SC*, II, 6)

This is Rousseau at the most pessimistic end of the spectrum. We might expect, once these concerns have been raised, for him to elaborate further on the self-regulating nature of the sovereign, or offer some firmer arguments for the inherent ability of a properly constituted sovereign body to ascertain and act on the general will. But instead he makes a very different move indeed:

> Both [individuals and the public] equally need guidance. Individuals must be obliged to subordinate their will to their reason; the public must be taught to recognise what it desires. [. . .] Hence the necessity of a lawgiver. (*SC*, II, 6)

This is something entirely new. We will now turn to see what Rousseau intends by introducing this unfamiliar element into the mix, and whether it succeeds in solving the problem of the sovereign's reliability we have been considering thus far.

The lawgiver (7, 12)

Rousseau claims that in order to discover the rules of society, it is necessary for the multitude to be guided by a superior intellect, someone of such perspicacity and discernment that the general will is as clear to them as it is faint and indistinct to normal mortals. The qualities required by such a figure are truly remarkable: he must understand the emotions and desires of ordinary people without being subject to them himself; he must concern himself with the happiness of the masses while being indifferent to it in person; and must be wholly familiar with human nature but nonetheless incapable of being corrupted by it.[10] These qualities seem like something only an alien or a deity could possess, and indeed Rousseau indicates that there is something divine about the lawgiver and his mission. At the least, the lawgiver is an exceptional individual, a unique genius capable of perceiving the best course for a given community. He is also described as the founder of such societies, the original man of vision who sets the community on the path towards a stable future, and without whom the transition from inequality to equality is doomed.

Thus introduced, the lawgiver seems a bizarre departure from the argument Rousseau has been making up until now. Previously, when he has attempted to show that his political order holds the promise of freedom and equality, he has seemed to indicate that the institutions themselves (state and sovereign) working in a suitably defined manner are all that is needed. Any justification he has offered for this vision has generally been along the lines that human nature is such that *The Social Contract* and its resultant organizations will enable people by themselves to construct a political system free from inequality and oppression. Now, however, it seems necessary to impose an external force, and one which, on the face of it, looks outlandish in the extreme. Rousseau acknowledges this apparent difficulty. If even great princes are rare, he admits, how much rarer will the lawgiver figure be? However, the reason the lawgiver has to be so rarely gifted is that his task is of the highest magnitude. It falls to him to endow the people he is responsible for with the qualities they need to prosper and develop. It is the lawgiver who enables individuals to move from the strife of the state of nature into civil society. In order to do this, Rousseau says, he must first strip away the pre-existent powers which all individuals have, and replace them with the necessary skills to embrace and maintain the society of *The Social Contract*. In essence, therefore, the lawgiver's job is to mould and shape people so that, when placed in the correct institutional setting, they will be competent to discern the general will and act upon it. Without his actions, there can be no lasting transition from the state of nature to the ideal society.

It would perhaps be natural, looking at the powers and role of the lawgiver, to assume that he would occupy a place at the head of the society. This, however, would be in contradiction to Rousseau's earlier insistence that the sovereign power is the highest authority in his political scheme. So the lawgiver occupies a rather peculiar position in Rousseau's institutional framework. Despite his name, he can pass no laws of his own (these would of course be partial, emanating as they do from an individual will, however rarefied). He has no particular place in the constitution of the society, and has no special sanction to command other members of the state. By way of an exemplar for such a figure, Rousseau cites Lycurgus, the ruler of ancient Sparta, who is said to have renounced his monarchical functions in order to endow his fellow citizens with laws. Placing the powers of both sovereign and lawgiver in the same hands would be disastrous, according to Rousseau, so the two functions must be kept entirely separate.

So what does the lawgiver actually do? His key task, we are told, is to 'frame' the laws, and guide the sovereign such that the pronouncements it passes are wise and efficacious. However, the way he does this is rather curious. Rousseau claims that he will be unable to persuade the potential citizens of the state to adopt a suitable set of attitudes and norms through reasoned argument. This is because, prior to the advent of civil society and the enlightening effects of civil liberty, the multitudes can have only a dim appreciation of the subtleties of the lawgiver's potential arguments. For the lawgiver to attempt to shape the behaviour of the masses through reason would be as pointless as a learned sage speaking to an uneducated crowd in the jargon of the academy: his argument would simply be lost. Neither, though, can the lawgiver use force to achieve his ends, and we already know that he cannot directly pass laws himself. So he must resort to inspiring the people to assume the proper attitudes and social spirit via an indirect mechanism and, in some way, 'persuade without convincing'.

Essentially, this means that the bulk of the populace must be led to see the wisdom and prudence of the lawgiver's proposed legal framework without ever being explicitly asked to accept the truth of what he says. To see what Rousseau means here, consider how other non-explicit means of persuasion work. In the cinema, for example, a film often has a 'message': a moral argument which it wishes to make. However, most such films do not take the form of a propositional argument in which the audience is invited to accept the truth of the conclusion from the truth of the premises. Instead, a skilled director will make their moral message seem apparent by exciting emotional responses in the right places. The audience may leave the cinema fully persuaded that the moral message is correct, and determine to live their lives more closely in accordance with it, but they have not explicitly considered the argument in its raw state, nor formally acquiesced to its truth. Similarly, we can see the same effects at work in music, drama and literature: Dickens does not *argue* that generosity and charity are virtues to be imitated; instead, he attempts to show the reader, through the sufferings of Scrooge, that the selfish receive their just deserts in the end. This method of showing by analogy or example is a very widespread technique in social education, and is obviously instrumental in passing moral attitudes to children.[11]

It is this form of persuasion that the lawgiver must resort to in order to shape the society towards the right end. But he does not do so simply by appealing to emotions; rather, in Rousseau's account he is to present himself as a kind of interpreter of the divine will, such that the people believe his wisdom is that of the gods. Not everyone can pull such a trick off: for the unskilled practitioner, the attempt will end in ignominy when the ruse is uncovered. A dishonest pretender who attempted to pull the wool over people's eyes for no higher purpose may succeed in the short term, but could only ever string together a community of the weak-minded, and the resultant social order would not last long. The lawgiver has two important attributes which prevent this fate happening to him. First, he has the genuine interests of the multitude at heart: through his supernatural forbearance, he is able to dupe the entire prospective community with only the potential reward of seeing them elevated into a superior state of social harmony to motivate him. Second, he has the skills of rhetoric and persuasion needed to convince even the stoutest and most upright of people that his recommendations are genuinely of divine origin, and risks no uncovering of his mission or exposure of the deception.

The object of all this chicanery is to encourage the populace, which would otherwise be prey to the divergent ambitions of their individual wills, to consider themselves part of a shared project, one in which they can genuinely feel themselves a part, and which they have no reason to stymie by pursuing a partial set of interests. For Rousseau, this is in the end the copper-bottomed guarantee that the sovereign of his proposed state will refrain from abusing its position of absolute power. Instead of external sanctions, the populace will be led by the lawgiver to feel themselves as a single entity with a single set of goals and objectives, and will willingly be sculpted into a united corporate block, free of dissension and willing only the common good.

It is not hard, given such an account, to raise objections to the introduction of the lawgiver. For many commentators, it is the least persuasive part of Rousseau's entire picture. At first glance, it may appear to be nothing more than a rather clumsy solution to the problem of the reliability of the sovereign: almost literally, a *deus ex machina* of the first order. The most obvious worry will be over the seemingly boundless capabilities of such an individual. Although Rousseau nods towards the rarity of suitable candidates, it might well be felt that the impressive list of attributes he lists for the lawgiver would be impossible to find in the real world. We may be reminded of Plato's Philosopher Kings, over which similar worries have been raised. Indeed, it rather gives the lie to his promise, right at the beginning of *The Social Contract*, to take men 'as they are', rather than idealized versions of them. The problem is made worse by the fact that, in addition to having an implausible degree of selflessness and philanthropy, the lawgiver also needs to have a very highly attuned understanding of how political systems work, and to know the best course of action to take for their sound establishment. But if the lawgiver is a condition for the establishment of a properly regulated society, how do lawgivers themselves ever become possible? Presumably, only someone with experience of how a justly ordered society works would be able to guide the ignorant masses into the light of reason, but no such societies could emerge without a pre-existent body of lawgivers to steer them into being. It seems like the classic 'chicken and egg' situation: lawgivers are necessary to bring about well-ordered civil society, but the skills lawgivers possess could only come from experience of such civil society.

Even if we could resolve the practical question of where lawgivers come from and how they get their unique abilities, there is a further question of how well the very notion fits in with Rousseau's scheme as previously expounded. As we know, one of the touchstones of Rousseau's enterprise is the issue of equality. For him, genuine freedom is only possible when all members of the community relinquish their rights and powers to a common pool, and from that point onwards participate as equals in the deliberations of the sovereign body. Should an individual or group rise to a position of particular prominence within the state, such that the direction of the whole is influenced by their partial will, then the very essence of the social pact is undone. Even if the lawgiver is proscribed from passing laws himself, does not the fact that he has a uniquely privileged role in the evolution of the state clash with this objective of equality? The very fact that he has extra information about the goals of the society which are unknown to the majority seems to give him an edge, and the fact that he surreptitiously pushes the entire populace in a direction of his choosing apparently undermines one of Rousseau's core ideas, that there are no classes of people more fitted to rule by nature than others.

These are serious objections to the figure of the lawgiver. As presented in the text, he *does* seem to be an individual of almost comical super-powers, who also stands uncomfortably apart from the general spirit of communal equality which vitiates Rousseau's political scheme. Arguably, however, these apparent absurdities can be addressed by reconstructing Rousseau's thoughts somewhat, albeit at the price of modifying his most colourful claims for the lawgiver's powers. The important feature to observe is that the lawgiver's role is principally to guide the populace from the state of nature into civil society. Once this state has been achieved, it is not necessarily the case that his role continues in the same form thereafter. When the masses have been enlightened, there is no longer a need for an individual lawgiver, since the society as a whole will have come to see themselves as a single entity with shared goals and goods, and under such conditions the sovereign will much more reliably pick out and act upon the general will. As such, Rousseau's objective of equality within the state of *The Social Contract* is maintained: though the populace needs to be kick-started by the god-like lawgiver, once they have moved into the correct institutional framework, and have the right set of motivations, the lawgiver can melt once more into the crowd, his work done. Thereafter, we might suppose that things have as good a chance as they ever will of proceeding smoothly, with all constituents of the state on a genuinely equal basis and operating from an appropriately enlightened platform.

Similarly, the somewhat outrageous claims for the abilities of the lawgiver can perhaps be modified slightly with little loss. A more sober vision of the situation might be this. The transition from the state of nature to civil society is hard. Even though the long-term benefits of such a shift are considerable, such distant rewards will be difficult to appreciate for most, and the likelihood is that, in the absence of an exceptional leader, the transition will never be made. However, from time to time, such geniuses do emerge. Lycurgus would be a key example for Rousseau, but there are plenty of other

historical figures who have seemingly individually altered the fundamental principles of the communities in which they have been born
through force of will and the attraction of their message (Jesus,
Mohammed, Lenin, etc.). The essential quality these leaders have in
abundance is an ability to enthuse and motivate the masses around
them such that major social and cultural change can occur. This ability does not lie so much in rational argument, but in a somewhat
unquantifiable capability to rally otherwise disparate groups into a
cohesive whole. It may remain unlikely that such a figure will emerge,
but it is not impossible. And if one of these inspirational characters
can grasp the benefit of the social order which Rousseau proposes,
then the possibility of such a political system being realized is greatly
enhanced.

Presented thus, the notion of the lawgiver is little more than the
'Great Man' idea common in politics and history. We can, if we
choose, see Rousseau as simply making the point that no social
change comes about without the agency of exceptional individuals.
If such individuals restrict their role to the formation of the social
order, and refrain from seizing power themselves once the institutions are up and running, then there is less ground of conflict between
this idea and the egalitarian tenor of Rousseau's wider picture. And
even though the qualities needed by the lawgiver are extraordinary,
geniuses *do* appear from time to time: the trick is to make the most of
the opportunity when it arises.

This is, perhaps, as sympathetic a reading as one can make. But for
those already opposed to Rousseau's general project, the lawgiver
will no doubt still seem a chimerical and implausible add-on. If the
price of rendering his institutional framework coherent and morally
acceptable is the addition of a quasi-divine showman, then that may
be taken as proof that the system is fatally flawed. After all, almost
any political scheme could be rendered more acceptable with the
addition of such a knowledgeable guiding hand. And if one is already
disposed to find Rousseau's political order too close to totalitarianism for comfort, then the lawgiver will be additionally unacceptable.
His role, we have been told, is to deceive the populace into believing
that he is something of a divine emissary. Even if this deception is
being carried out for the good of the ignorant masses, a liberal critic
will find this institutionalized falsehood hard to justify. There have
been too many occasions in history when governments have lied to
their citizens 'for their own good', and where the consequences have

been predictably tragic. It will seem to many that the lawgiver's activities as described by Rousseau are nothing short of sanctioned lying, and whatever skills he may possess, this is always unjust and liable to result in despotism.

We also need to consider a final criticism of the nature of the lawgiver's work, which concerns the morality of altering the fundamental character of people in the first place. If we set aside for a moment the worries over the lawgiver's extraordinary skills and the acceptability of his methods, we are still left with a situation where the basic nature of the populace is being subtly changed, and moreover without their consent. As we saw earlier in our discussion of civil liberty, Rousseau thinks that the transition from the state of nature to civil society brings about a remarkable transformation in people. We now know a little more about this change: they are moved from being creatures with a strong sense of individual autonomy and purpose, and transformed into citizens of a state with a shared vision and communal purpose. This process is called 'denaturing', and is a major theme running throughout Rousseau's wider work. In *Émile*, he describes the process thus:

> Good social institutions are those which best know how to denature man, to take his absolute existence from him in order to give him a relative one and transport the I into the common unity, with the result that each individual believes himself no longer one but a part of the unity and no longer feels himself except within the whole.[12]

This is the lawgiver's objective. We have considered the reasons why such a goal might be desirable: it makes the sovereign less prone to the distortion of its members' partial wills and enables it to tune more closely into the general will. But denaturing might be thought a high price to pay for this result. For the critic of Rousseau, it is easy to see the act of denaturing as a sinister stripping away of all genuine individual autonomy in favour of a blind, supine subservience to an impartial communal will. The spontaneity, variety and self-mastery of individuals is, for many people, one of humanity's essential moral features, the loss of which would render any political system reprehensible. With the experience of the twentieth century behind us, we may be very suspicious of any political project which has the goal of subsuming a sense of personal independence into an overarching social objective.

Once again, our view on this matter is likely to be coloured by the level of sympathy we have with Rousseau's conception of human nature. To recall, Rousseau is very sceptical of the potential of success for individuals acting as independent agents within the confines of a materially interdependent society. The benign drive of *amour de soi* is liable in such an environment to degenerate into a malign form of *amour-propre*, in which conflicting individual wills are forever set against one another in an endless struggle for mastery. If people are unable to see the common good with any reliability, then society will remain a place of frustration and inequality, and the natural potential human beings have for happiness and fulfilment will stay elusive. Rousseau's solution to this state, as we have seen, is for those individuals to contract away their personal freedoms in exchange for a superior communal version. But in practice each individual only really gives away the right to act upon issues which all their fellows have an equal common interest in: safety, security, moral significance, etc. And the regular act of participation in the social order – voting in the sovereign body – is by its nature only concerned with such general objectives, not the minutiae of each individual's entire life. So a sympathizer with Rousseau's general aims could argue here that denaturing only amounts to this: an individual, acting in their capacity as a citizen, coming to see no real difference between their own interests and those of the state as a whole. And the positive results of such a realization outweigh any objections we may have over the legitimacy of the transformation.[13]

The fitness of nations (8–11)

Whether or not one is in accordance with Rousseau on this point, it is worth noting that his close attention to the need for a suitable sense of cultural identity and shared moral purpose is one of the most radical and perceptive aspects of *The Social Contract*. Much political science and political philosophy concentrates on the structure of society: its institutions, constitution and laws. Such things are obviously of great importance to the success of any theory, and the care Rousseau takes to try and delineate the functions of sovereign, state and other layers of administration illustrates that he is perfectly aware of this. But he also spends a great deal of time in thinking about what kind of moral vision and cultural make-up is required to exploit the structural aspects of society effectively. After all, a community which systematically hated itself and was constantly seeking only the destruction of the things its constituents stood for would not prosper even if, structurally speaking, it was organized in the most efficient way possible. Rousseau is surely correct to point out that there needs to be some kind of communal vision and sense of shared endeavour to animate the institutions of state properly.

However, there are ways of generating a social vision which are more or less acceptable. A society united by a strong sense of racial superiority may exhibit the cohesiveness Rousseau envisages, but perhaps at the price of its moral character and long-term sustainability. In the remaining chapters of Book II, Rousseau offers some thoughts on what kinds of societies, in a cultural and environmental sense, are capable of being turned into the ideal civil community he advocates. Perhaps surprisingly given much of what he has said previously, he by no means thinks that every culture or nation is fit to be guided by the lawgiver into an ideal political order. The ingredients needed for the great transformation are not uniformly present either geographically or temporally. In the latter case especially, Rousseau thinks that great care needs to be taken over whether a nation is mature enough to accept the rigours of a move into true civil liberty. If done too soon, then the populace may be unable to take advantage of the message of the lawgiver, and the edifice constructed will be weak and liable to dissolution. If done too late, then the alternative social system may be so entrenched that no change is possible. The lawgiver is a powerful persuader, but he is not an alchemist: the material he works with must be capable of being refined.

This seems somewhat at odds with the tone of Rousseau's project as announced at the beginning of *The Social Contract*. There are two areas where we may feel that the situation has altered. First, Rousseau earlier appeared to advocate the universal appeal and possibility of his social order taking root. If man is everywhere in chains, then a reasonable expectation of his project, which claims to show how such a situation can be made legitimate, would be that it holds the promise of liberation for all such men, and that fetters are capable of being broken everywhere. Now it seems that only some peoples are made of the right stuff to be able to throw off their shackles: by implication, that means that some are stuck with the status quo, at least until such time as their capabilities evolve.

This qualification risks ruining much of the appeal of Rousseau's project, at least if the criteria for transformation are too high or demanding. In the remainder of Book II, he outlines what these must be. An important first consideration is the size of the community. For Rousseau, small states are better than large ones, since, among other things, the former are much better at sustaining the sense of community and shared purpose which the lawgiver inculcates. Even in the modern world, where rapid and easy communication is widespread, it is easy to see why this consideration is important for Rousseau. The sovereign body, composed of all members of the state, needs to meet and deliberate in order for the general will to be enacted. This would be difficult in a large and diffuse nation, whereas in a small one such problems are less acute. Moreover, in an environment where each citizen has a reasonable chance of knowing most of the others, or at least being familiar with the circumstances which affect them all, then the lawgiver's urgings will seem more plausible.

A second and more important consideration is the cultural homogeneity of the populace. For Rousseau, the only people who are capable of being given laws (in the proper sense) are those who have already been bound together in some form of covenant or union, but who have not developed a legal system of the normal sort. In other words, they must have some kind of prior means of self-identification, but must not have advanced far enough along the road of civilization to have allowed poorly constituted practices to crystallize. In addition to these major considerations, Rousseau also thinks that a host of other factors conspire to frustrate the efforts of the lawgiver, such as too many riches (or too much poverty), too much cohesion (or too little) and bellicosity (or feebleness). At the end of the passage where many of these criteria are laid down (*SC*, II, 10), he seems at his most pessimistic about the possibility of his reforms, and implies that the only country in Europe of his time capable of meeting his conditions is Corsica.[14]

Even if we take this pessimism with a pinch of salt (elsewhere he is much more phlegmatic), it certainly seems the case that, for Rousseau, the lawgiver must pick his subjects carefully, and there is no guarantee that every nation has what it takes to enter into a legitimate and equal contractual social arrangement. Of all the various things which must be in place, the most important is the prior sense of community and shared union: it is this which the lawgiver can work on to help the community move smoothly into Rousseau's institutional framework. But this insistence on an existing sense of being bound together raises the second area of difference with what has gone before. To recall, one of Rousseau's objections to Grotius's idea that a nation could be formed when a group of individuals decided to give themselves up to a monarch was that the individuals, by the act of coming together and deliberating towards a common goal, had already become a people, and the presence of a monarch was therefore otiose. And yet, it seems that a precondition of Rousseau's own political system is that there is something like a shared sense of community already in place. His earlier implication, that the state of *The Social Contract* emerges from a previous poorly formed set of institutions in which malign *amour-propre* has taken its toll, now seems to have been replaced by the idea that the lawgiver must intervene in the earlier stages of social development, before bad practices have gone too far. Indeed, in a characteristic sound bite, he confidently announces that 'nations, like men, are teachable only in their youth; with age they become incorrigible' (*SC*, II, 8).

These inconsistencies are irritating, and together have the effect of undermining confidence in the rigour of Rousseau's vision. We are left at the end of Book II with considerable uncertainty over the precise sequence of events required to turn a body of people into the ideal civil society, or the exact set of circumstances under which such a transformation can occur. However, given Rousseau's promise to deal with men 'as they are', perhaps we should not be too surprised that his ambitious project oscillates somewhat between the harsh practicalities of the real world and the more rarefied air of theoretical state-building. What these final chapters of Book II do give us is a recognition by Rousseau of the practical challenges involved in applying his scheme to the vagaries and imperfections of the real world. In the following two Books, he does have a little more to say about all of these issues, but the bulk of his political project at the fundamental level – the setting out of the basic principles of his society – has now been laid out. So we should turn to a summary of the ideas we have covered so far, and see if a convincing political scheme has emerged.

SUMMARY

Rousseau has described a society in which every member surrenders their individual freedom to the community as a whole. They do this in order to gain the security of being part of a larger entity, and to escape the dangers of the state of nature and the inequality of poorly constituted social orders. As a citizen, they are then bound by the laws emanating from the sovereign body, and have no reserved rights with which to challenge or reject such laws. But they are also a member of the sovereign, and thus have a say in how those laws are drafted. Since all fellow citizens are also in the same situation, Rousseau believes that the body will respect the safety and interests of its members in a more reliable way than an alternative system relying on a constitutional separation between the rulers and the ruled.

The laws the sovereign passes are by their nature general: they may not pinpoint individuals or interest groups either positively or negatively. Properly formulated, these laws will also reflect the general will of the community. This notion is derived from the collected individual wills of all the members of the sovereign body through a rational consideration of the best outcome for the state as a whole. When the sovereign body votes, the matter is settled. In such a situation, if the sovereign is acting appropriately, then the resultant statement of the general will be a reliable, impartial guide to the continued prosperity of the society.

However, it is possible, even likely, that the sovereign may misinterpret the general will, or choose to ignore it. In order to prevent this eventuality, the community must be so constituted that its members learn to cultivate a genuine sense of a shared enterprise, and are taught to equate their own interests with that of the state. There is no guarantee that such vision will be possible in every nation. It may be necessary for a person of great vision to guide the rest of the members of the state towards that realization. In this case, the qualities needed by such a person would be remarkable, and the populace also of an appropriately receptive nature to benefit from their instruction. Should all unfold thus, however, then each constituent individual will benefit from an enjoyment of 'civil liberty', and be free of the chains that formerly bound them. The deliberations of the sovereign will be reliable, and the resultant social order will guarantee both freedom and equality.

Such is, in very brief outline, the scheme we have been discussing. It is by no means a complete statement of Rousseau's political views: we have yet to consider his conception of the subordinate level of government at all (which is the subject of Book III, the largest division of *The Social Contract*), and there are further important ideas expressed in Book IV. Nonetheless, we are perhaps for the first time able to return to the two questions we raised in the previous chapter concerning the acceptability of his political vision:

1. Is the model coherent and conceptually sound? Can the central ideas be expressed clearly with no ambiguity or contradiction?
2. If so, what would be the practical consequences of such a society? Most importantly, would it really deliver the benefits Rousseau desires: freedom for all, and the flourishing of human potential?

With regard to the first issue, we may feel that, at least as laid down in the text of *The Social Contract*, there are areas where Rousseau's thought is more than a little opaque. Certainly, many of his critics have been quick to write it off as a hopeless muddle. Nonetheless, it has seemed to other more sympathetic readers that there is a coherent narrative there to be picked out, especially if one takes the time to develop a proper appreciation of Rousseau's psychological theory and the motivation behind it. In this guide we have generally followed the order of chapters as they are found in the text itself, and it seems to me that, for all its pockets of fog, there is a vision running through *The Social Contract* which remains reasonably consistent, and which generates a political scheme which one can engage with fruitfully. There is of course much controversy over the correct (or perhaps most coherent) interpretation of the general will, and the unhappy brevity of Rousseau's descriptions of its derivation from the will of all must be counted as a major blow to the credibility of the project. We will return to some of these issues in the final chapter of this book.

The second issue, concerning the practical consequences of Rousseau's state, is similarly vexed. It does not help that such a society has never been realized, leaving the question open as to how a sovereign power constituted along Rousseau's lines might actually function. In looking to the real world, the most similar exemplars have yielded verdicts as diverse as the motivations of Rousseau's many commentators. He may be seen as an advocate of progressive social democracy just as much as the father of totalitarianism. Again, we will have cause to look a little closer at these varied responses in our final chapter. There should be no doubt that Rousseau's ideas have had an enormous influence on the development of real political systems, even if they have never been adopted in their totality. However, since we still have much to learn about the practical workings of the civil state and of Rousseau's thoughts on the most efficient and just mechanisms of administration, we should turn now to Book III, where some of the more practical aspects of his thought are expounded.

STUDY QUESTIONS

1. What are the key characteristics of the sovereign body? Why must it have these attributes?
2. Give an account of the general will, paying attention to its derivation from the will of all.
3. What constraints are there on the activities of the sovereign power, according to Rousseau? Are these sufficient to prevent the abuse of individual members of the state?
4. Describe the nature and function of the lawgiver in Rousseau's political scheme. How successful is the introduction of this element in solving the problems presented by his theory?
5. In Rousseau's view, what are the prior ingredients needed for a people to be such that they are fit to receive laws? Why does Rousseau insist on these qualities?

BOOKS III AND IV

The second half of *The Social Contract* concentrates on Rousseau's thoughts concerning the practicalities of government, rather than the most fundamental constitutional underpinnings of the state. Devoted as it is to concrete issues of governance and efficiency, there is much in Books III and IV which may seem to the modern reader either obscure or of interest only to historians of political thought. Certainly, Rousseau's practical vision of government has not been as influential as his ideas on the basis of a just society. Nonetheless, there are important claims made by Rousseau in his concluding sections about the relationship between the sovereign and the people, the consequences for society when social institutions begin to break down, the best types of administration, and the role of religion. It was particularly this last topic, introduced right at the end of *The Social Contract*, which was to get Rousseau in so much trouble with the authorities.

The government (III, 1–2)

As we have seen, in Rousseau's scheme the sovereign body is the legislative organ of the state. It passes general, fundamental laws which bind all members of the community. The sovereign has no business acting on those laws itself, or passing decrees which pick out individuals or interest groups within the state. As such, it would not be reasonable to expect the sovereign to sit in judgement on every issue facing the community. Some matters would require a degree of partiality which the sovereign cannot consider, some would necessitate taking action rather than legislation, and some would simply be of insufficient importance to drag every member of the community to an assembly of all. What is needed is an subordinate body charged with implementing the many administrative matters for which the sovereign body is unsuited. This is what Rousseau has in mind for the institution of government.

Rousseau sets up his discussion of this new body using the analogy, once again, of the body. Just as an individual person has separate faculties for willing (the mind) and acting (the body), so the body politic has separate faculties for creating legislation and acting in accordance with it. According to Rousseau, the executive faculty always involves direction towards a definite object, so can never work in accordance with the general will. Instead, government should be thought of as the institution which pulls the citizens of the state together and ensures that the laws passed by the sovereign are followed. It is also described by Rousseau as an 'intermediary' between the supreme power (the sovereign) and the populace. Rousseau makes it clear that he is using the term in his own, somewhat specialized, sense here. If his description of government seems a little counter-intuitive, he notes, then that is because the terms 'sovereign' and 'government' are often used as counterparts with no distinction made between them. In Rousseau's project, they have different roles and constitutions, and he is careful to distinguish his use of terms. When he talks of magistrates, kings, princes or governors, he is referring to various offices of the government, and not of a supreme head of state in a way which we might be familiar with. However grand the title, no member of the government is ever for Rousseau more than an official of the sovereign body, exercising a kind of 'commission' on behalf of the general assembly of the entire community. Furthermore, however much power to enact laws a sovereign chooses to delegate to the government, this decision may be rescinded at any time. Unlike the social contract, which is made once at the beginning of the life of the state and is thereafter irrevocable, the activities of the community in creating a government are open to revision in the light of experience.

Having sketched the relationship between the two bodies, Rousseau then gives his views on the optimal size of the government. Unhappily, this discussion is couched in geometrical terms which seem to do little to clarify his ideas. When reading the text here, the essential thing to bear in mind is that he thinks there is a simple relationship between the relative sizes of the state and the government which changes as the absolute size of the population shrinks or falls. By way of example, he considers a society with 10,000 citizens. When these are called together into a sovereign assembly, each individual's vote is only worth 1/10,000 of the whole. As such, they have a relatively small input into the deliberations which determine the general will. This discrepancy is a matter of some concern, since it is important for the cohesion of the state that every member feels properly involved in the deliberations of the sovereign. If the state were to enlarge rapidly, then the share of the sovereign constituted by each citizen would fall further. The further this process continues, the less each individual will naturally feel attuned to the general will. If the enlargement reaches a point where the dictates of the general will are very abstracted from the dictates of each individual's partial will, then force may be required on a regular basis to ensure that all follow the law. The action of forcing an individual or a group to comply with a sovereign ruling falls to the government, and so its numbers would have to increase proportionately. As the dictates of the general will become less surely perceived by the populace, the number of magistrates, who are charged with enforcing the laws of the sovereign, must rise to ensure that any recusants will be forced to be free.

Once again, we may feel rather uneasy with the direction of this argument. If the demands of the general will are weak, then the expansion of the enforcing arm of the state seems a somewhat brutal response to ensure that everyone keeps in line. After all, we have been told that the ideal situation for Rousseau's community is the fostering of a sense of shared vision and values, such that coercion will over time cease to be the major driver of compliance with the sovereign's decisions. If it were otherwise, then the promise of freedom, the cornerstone of Rousseau's system, seems to have become distant once more. Rousseau is alive to this worry, and notes that the larger and more powerful the government becomes, the more the temptation on the part of the magistrates will grow to abuse their role. The solution to this is to ensure that the sovereign retains equivalent powers to strip the magistrates of their position should they fail to carry out the laws diligently and impartially. Once again he illustrates this point with examples taken from mathematical ratios, and comes up with the ideal recipe for success: the size of the government should always be the square root of the size of the sovereign. If these proportions obtain, then the respective objectives of social compliance and sovereign oversight will be as guaranteed as is possible, and the state will be a harmonious one.

It is difficult to take Rousseau's precise prescription here entirely seriously. In particular, there seems little reason to accept his faith that simple mathematical ratios will yield an ideal balance between sovereign and government sizes with any reliability. However, his point about the relative sizes and influence of the sovereign and government is important. If the magistrates become the true driver of the community's policies then the general will can no longer be said to be animating the community as it should. On the other hand, practicality demands that there be an effective executive arm to ensure that every citizen complies with the just laws of the sovereign assembly. The problem is how to balance those two important factors in such a way that the principles of the general will as outlined in the previous two books are not violated.

A key difficulty is, as Rousseau notes, that the government will tend to develop a sense of its own identity over time, and will increasingly see itself as a separate body to the state considered in its entirety. Once this happens, then the community is in danger of fracturing into factions, and the entire social project is placed in jeopardy. Rousseau characterizes the issue thus. Each member of the government has three 'wills', or motivations. The first is their individual will, which every member of the community possesses. The second is their will as a magistrate, what Rousseau calls their 'corporate will'. The third is their general will. Unfortunately, in Rousseau's estimation the strengths of these three drives will normally be in inverse proportion to their social usefulness: for any single magistrate, their individual will is generally the strongest, followed by their corporate will, with their general will trailing behind. The problem of an over-mighty government may therefore be expressed as the problem of the corporate will eclipsing the general will, and the interests of the faction of magistrates replacing the interests of all as the guiding principle of the community. It is important to note here that Rousseau is not introducing a special new notion when he refers to the 'corporate will'. Just as the 'will of all' is Rousseau's term for the collected individual wills of the state, the corporate will is the name given to the collected individual wills of all the magistrates. In terms of each individual magistrate, their corporate will is the motivation to see a certain course of action take place while considering their role *as* magistrates. Their general will, by contrast, is what they desire to happen while considering their role as members of the state.

Once more, this problem is exacerbated if the government is the wrong size. Rousseau gives the example of the government being constituted by a single person. In this case, the difference between the sole magistrate's individual will and the corporate will is zero. This has the advantage that the actions of the government will tend to be swift and decisive: there is no constitutional requirement for the magistrate to consult any external advisers, and the process of deliberation will therefore be easy. On the other hand, since the general will is naturally the weaker of the three considerations driving the magistrate's actions, there is little chance that the activities of the government will reliably correspond closely to the optimal course for the whole community as laid down by the sovereign. Moreover, the tendency of the magistrate to see himself as separate from the remainder of the citizens will be very strong in such a scenario. At the other end of the scale, Rousseau considers the case of *all* members of the state being magistrates. This has the effect of aligning the corporate will very closely with the general will, and limiting the scope for the government to consider itself apart from the sovereign. Importantly, the prospect of factionalism – ever a worry for Rousseau – recedes. However, in this situation the virtues of swift and decisive executive force have been lost, and we have returned to the practical problem of a political system in which every decision, of whatever nature, needs the involvement of all citizens. Rousseau is conscious of the sluggishness and inefficiency of large administrative bodies, and remains consistently concerned that the functions of the government and the sovereign are kept separate.

So the question is one of balance. If the government is too big, then the pragmatic questions of governance become difficult; if too small, then the over-weaning corporate will poses severe tests for the coherence of the community and its continuing adherence to the properly ascertained general will. The need for larger societies to keep their citizens in line gives a reason to increase the number of magistrates, while the drift towards corruption or factionalism posed by the corporate will gives a reason to reduce it. These look like sensible worries, and so we might expect Rousseau here to give a more detailed account of how the correct proportions of government and sovereign are to be derived. However, aside from the quasi-geometrical considerations we have already come across, he concludes at the end of Chapter 2 that the job of deciding how big the government should be falls to the lawgiver, whose art it is to decide on the number of magistrates most suited to the size of the population. This may seem rather unsatisfactory, since the government's role is an important one: it mediates between the state and the sovereign, and has the responsibility for enacting whatever powers are placed in its hands by the assembly of all citizens. Rousseau has identified a key problem with the constitution of such a body: how should its size and power be determined, given the potential pitfalls of getting it wrong? The answer, perhaps disappointingly, seems to be that the omniscient lawgiver will once more step into the breach to ensure that all is ordered as it should be.

This, taken together with the idiosyncratic mathematical basis for the ideal number of magistrates, may make Rousseau's account of government seem rather speculative and unconvincing. However, in mitigation, his objectives for *The Social Contract* should be borne in mind. Even in Book III, he is principally concerned with the fundamental principles of the social order, not the detail of their implementation. Throughout the text, he attempts to expound a constitutional framework in which citizens may enjoy both freedom and equality. Given the length of his treatise and his desire to remain at a somewhat abstract theoretical level, it is perhaps inevitable that some of the practicalities of his scheme remain to be worked out even when the framework is completed. Additionally, the lawgiver, whom as we have seen is responsible for the genesis of the state and its progression towards a suitable culture of communal vision, is already playing a large role in the formation of its institutions, and so the extension of this to include a decision over the make-up of the government is perhaps to be expected. In any case, Rousseau believes that the question of the ideal constitution of government is more complicated than the issue of the respective sizes of the state and its magistrates. Given the variety of cultures and environments in existence, there may be more than one type of government which holds the promise of implementing the sovereign's laws effectively. Over the next five chapters he considers the implications of various types of administration, and it is this discussion to which we now turn.

Types of government (III, 3–8)

Rousseau distinguished three basic types of government. First, if the entire populace forms the government, then this is democracy. The system is also democratic if a majority of the citizens are also members of the government: the important thing is that citizen magistrates outnumber citizen non-magistrates. Second, if a small number of citizens form the government, then the system is an aristocracy. Finally, if a single individual takes charge of the mechanisms of government such that all other officials of the state in some way take their orders from them, then the system is a monarchy. Rousseau would have been familiar, either directly or through his historical studies, with the example of all three: France was a monarchy in which all power flowed downwards from the king; Geneva was something of a cross between a democracy and an aristocratic oligarchy; and the classical exemplars of Athens and Sparta furnished further evidence, for Rousseau, of the efficacy of various different models. As we shall see, Rousseau by no means thinks that democracy, at least in its most direct form, is the type of government best suited for his ideal state, despite the democratic nature of the sovereign body. To some extent, the particular environmental circumstances of the nation in question determine the issue: Rousseau concludes Chapter 3 with the remark that, in general, democracy suits small states, aristocracy medium ones and monarchy large ones. He also thinks there are plenty of circumstances in which the systems may admit of being mixed, or where exceptions to the rule are preferable. Despite all these caveats, after considering each in turn, we shall see that one system emerges the clear winner.

Rousseau starts his consideration of the merits of different systems with democracy. He notes that it might seem obvious that a democratic form of government fits best with the political system he has previously outlined. After all, if the citizens of the state have all come together to formulate the laws, who could be better to pronounce on their application? Presumably, the members of the sovereign would have given some thought to the practical application of their legal proposals when considering the matter, so it would make sense for the business of government to be conducted by the same people who draw up the laws. However, Rousseau rejects this idea firmly. In his view, the actions of government, in which decisions may be given particular objects, corrode the impartiality of the sovereign, in which decisions may have no definite targets. Presumably, his worry is something to the effect that the ability of the average citizen to abstract themselves from their individual will while acting as a member of the sovereign body would be diminished if the same person were to play a similar role in the executive body, where no such abstraction is necessary. Once again, Rousseau is demonstrating a profound pessimism over the capacity of the average person to maintain a suitably objective attitude to the business of legislation. If the same people who formulate the laws are also responsible for their implementation, then they will be even less able to resist the pull of partial interests during the former process than usual.

In addition to this worry, Rousseau is very sceptical of the practical possibility of democracy. The very idea of having the bulk of the community involved in the business of administration seems to him unsustainable. Sooner or later, more focused members with a particular partial interest will assume a greater degree of control. As a result, democracy has the potential to usher in the factionalism which he so deplores. Moreover, the business of assembling the entire citizenry (or the bulk of them) to execute the business of government would be very difficult. Most nations would struggle to mobilize so many individuals frequently enough for the government to convene without terrible disruption to the smooth running of the state. As a result of this, for democracy to be a credible form of government, a number of specific conditions must obtain. First, the state must be small, so that the government may be readily assembled in a reasonable time. Second, the temperament of the people must be sufficiently amiable so that discussions are not needlessly prolonged or divisive. Third, the social status and material wealth of the assembled magistrates must be more or less the same. Fourth, the level of luxury must be relatively low, since Rousseau believes this will have an inevitably corrupting effect on the populace in a democracy. These conditions, taken together, look rather too onerous to be at all common. Indeed Rousseau's argument seems to be that such promising materials for the formation of a government are too good to be true. After all, if a society possessed such virtues in every member, what need would it have for government at all? Essentially, democracy, according to Rousseau, relies on the notion that people are more virtuous, self-controlled and well-intentioned than we have any right to expect, and thus it is an unrealistic candidate for a credible and successful form of government.

Given what has gone before concerning the nature of the sovereign, these views may be rather surprising. On the face of it, there seems little difference between the assembly of the sovereign body and the putative gathering of the democratic government: both require the state to mobilize all its citizens from time to time in order to pass laws or enact them. If this would prove too difficult in the case of government, how is it possible in the case of the sovereign? In addition, Rousseau's other practical objections to democratic administration seem contrived. The inability of people in general to abstract their role as a member of the sovereign from their role as a magistrate is a problem which affects all three types of government, and limiting the number of magistrates does not solve that by itself. In fact, Rousseau's real objection to democracy seems to be of a more general kind: that the demands of formulating the laws and administering them together create too much of a burden for the entire society (or the majority thereof). Given human frailty, the constant temptation for citizens to reject the general will and retreat into partiality, and the inability of disparate sections in a diverse society reliably to see themselves as part of the same project, democracy at the level of government is not something Rousseau thinks can ever work. If this rejection seems a bit too hasty, then it is worth bearing in mind that the form of democracy considered by Rousseau here is of a very direct nature. Unlike some modern democracies, where the involvement of the electorate is relatively infrequent and most decisions are taken on their behalf by a small set of representatives, Rousseau's target here is the idea that all decisions of note are taken by all members of the franchise. Such a form of government is indeed possible, but it is by no means the most widespread type of democracy found in the modern world.

In fact, what Rousseau calls 'aristocracy' turns out to be somewhat similar to the representative democracies with which a contemporary reader may be more familiar. By aristocracy in general, Rousseau means a small group of individuals charged by the sovereign with administering the business of government on its behalf. He starts his discussion of this form of administration by reminding the reader that the government is strictly subordinate to the sovereign: even if a group of citizens acquires a privileged role in the day-to-day running of the society, this activity is always subject to the mandate of the whole community, and the licence may be withdrawn at any time. He then considers three kinds of aristocratic system: natural, elective and hereditary. The first is analogous to the notion of natural sovereignty we considered in the first chapter: a body of people fitted to govern by virtue of their class, or nationality or racial origin. Rousseau, unsurprisingly, rejects this out of hand. He also rejects the hereditary principle, which he thinks is the worst of all possible forms of government. However, the elective model is one which he does think holds the promise of fair, effective administration. Under such a system, any member of the state has the potential to become a magistrate. Once the size of the government has been determined (the implication is that it will be relatively small), each position in the administration is filled by an election conducted according to rules drawn up by the sovereign. The resultant government has the advantage of practicality: a small body of magistrates will be able to fulfil its business with much less fuss than an unwieldy body comprising the majority of all citizens. Moreover, since the magistrates have been elected, rather than chanced upon through the vagaries of family relations or class, then there is a good chance that they will in fact be the best candidates for the job.

Rousseau acknowledges some difficulties with this situation. As he has already indicated, a small government runs the risk of deviating further from the general will than a big one. He also believes that aristocratic magistrates will be tempted to use their executive power to escape the demands of the law. Moreover, Rousseau thinks that the exalted position of the aristocrats will lead to material inequality. However, even though the potential for corruption is present, he claims that the character of the magistrates in an aristocracy is liable to be such that they will resist corruption more effectively than would the massed ranks of a democratic government. As Rousseau puts it, the virtues required on the part of the magistrates in an aristocracy may be onerous, but they are less unrealistic than those required to make a democratic government function. Because the magistrates have been elected, and such elections have taken place within the social order put in place by the lawgiver according to the proper functioning of the general will, there is at least the hope that the selected individuals will rule in a wise and beneficent manner.

As presented in the text, this situation may seem, once again, to be rather optimistic. In addition, it may appear that this structure of government fails to reflect Rousseau's consistent goal of equality, since a disproportionate amount of power is being wielded by a narrow group of individuals. However, two things should be remembered. First, since the task of government is to enact the will of the sovereign, the magistrates only have those powers which are given to them by the community as a whole. Though they have discretion over how to implement the laws of the state, they have no power to change them. Should their interpretation seem to the community to have departed from the general will in a systematic way, then the sovereign reserves the right to dissolve the government and reconvene it in another form. So in the sense that Rousseau thinks is important, the magistrates have no more rights than any other member of the state – they are still bound by the dictates of the general will and are subject to the laws agreed upon in the sovereign assembly. Second, the fact that the magistrates are elected under a system of suffrage devised by the sovereign gives the best possible chance, in an imperfect world, that they will be fitted to the job. In many respects, the model is similar to the kind of representative democracy we touched on above. Though the electorate in Rousseau's state may of course choose their magistrates badly or maliciously, the chances that they won't are much higher than in the case of hereditary or 'natural' selection. In addition, for Rousseau, the envisaged electoral activity takes place within a community which has had a strong sense of shared purpose and vision inculcated by the lawgiver, which gives extra reason to suppose that the citizens would make every effort to select the right candidates for government.[15]

It is evident from the text that this form of elected aristocracy is by far Rousseau's preferred system of government. However, for completeness' sake, he also discusses the third option, that of monarchy. The principal advantage of this system, according to Rousseau, is efficiency. Since a monarchical government is identical with a single individual, executive procedures and deliberations can take place quickly with minimal dissension. As all other officials of the government owe whatever powers they have to the monarch, the lines of command will be straightforward. As a result of this, monarchy is the form of government best suited to the administration of large or potentially unruly states. Whereas direct democracy may only flourish in small communities where the common interest is plainly to be seen and the logistics of frequent assembly are not too onerous, in diffuse territories the strong hand of monarchy is needed to maintain order and prevent the administration becoming sclerotic and inefficient. Rousseau also notes that there is nothing inherently in the notion of a monarchy which rules it out as a legitimate form of government for his ideal state. His earlier arguments against the rights of kings were with respect to their role as the potential sovereign of a nation. As in the case of aristocracy, under Rousseau's social scheme a king may, we should suppose, be perfectly capable of being deposed by the sovereign body of citizens if their rule departed systematically from the dictates of the general will.

This is, however, the limit of Rousseau's positive views on monarchy. Overwhelmingly, he is against the idea of a single individual assuming control of the functions of government. Some of the reasons for this we have already come across: if the individual will of the monarch coincides exactly with the corporate will of the government, then the legitimate general will would be muscled out, and the government will tend towards an extreme form of partiality. In the final analysis, according to Rousseau, human nature will always ensure that kings become overbearing and impatient with any restraint on their activities. They will come to see the mass of the populace as threats to their power, and accordingly seek to suppress sources of strength other than their own. The distance between the kings and their subjects will corrode the sense of joint purpose fostered by the lawgiver, and the social order will face a rapid degeneration into despotism. Though the demands of a large state do require a strong and efficient government, it is too much to expect that a single individual will remain consistently up to the task of presiding over the fractious citizenry without resorting to crude and oppressive methods. Finally, whereas the elective aristocratic system holds the promise of enhancing the moral character of the magistrates (since they have been selected by the populace on the basis of their fitness for office), the monarchical system tends to degrade the quality of the governmental officials. As the junior magistrates' position depends on patronage, the necessary character traits they possess will invariably be those of self-aggrandizement and obsequiousness.

The upstanding magistrates needed for the well-governed state, motivated by the common good and possessing the intellectual capability to administer the state effectively, are not cultivated by a monarchical system.

In the remainder of Chapter 6, Rousseau advances even more reasons for rejecting a monarchical government. It is perhaps natural that he should do so, given the political system in which he lived most of his life and the immediate audience for his political theory. The time he takes here to dispose of this option may however seem surprising, since he has already been at pains to reject monarchy as a suitable basis for the most important institution in the state – the sovereign – and the function of government carries much less authority and power. However, it is perfectly consistent of Rousseau to argue that his political scheme, which places so much emphasis on equality and the common good, is ill-suited to have the business of government placed in the hands of a single person. Given what Rousseau has consistently said about human nature, it is not surprising that he thinks the office of a monarch is basically incompatible with the constitutional framework he has outlined. Though he is careful not to rule the eventuality out entirely, it does seem right that the presence of an individual of very great power and influence sitting at the apex of an administrative system based on patronage and favour fits badly with the general tenor of *The Social Contract* taken as whole. Rousseau is surely right to think that the sovereign would have a hard job of restraining such a figure should they depart (as he expects they would) from the impartial demands of the general will. Though subordinate in power to the sovereign, the machinery of government is a very powerful tool, and it is easy to see how the two institutions could come into conflict.

So, for Rousseau, the ideal system of government is an elective aristocracy. This marries the efficiency of a small administration with the representative advantages of a democratic one. However, having established this, he then goes on to qualify the position somewhat. It would be too much to expect, he says, for governments in all cases to be pure examples of one type or another. Given the vagaries of different situations, it is likely that elements of one system may be used in another. Indeed, if for whatever reason a government were to assume too much power over the populace, then the sovereign may decide to deliberately dilute the purity of the administration. In a monarchical system, for example, the sovereign could vote to impose representative bodies with limited rights of veto over the monarch's actions. Similarly, an elective aristocracy could be established with different levels of authority within it, such that the most senior magistrates were more like monarchs, and the more junior, more like citizen members of a democratic assembly.

In addition to this muddying of the waters, Rousseau repeats his earlier claims on the environmental imperatives of government. We have already seen that small countries lend themselves to government at the democratic end of the spectrum, while larger ones demand one at the monarchical end. Rousseau further believes that such factors as climate, material wealth, ease of food production, culture and population all have an impact on the type of government best suited to the needs of the state. In language which is perhaps apt to seem naive to modern readers, he asserts that despotism is more liable to suit hot countries, barbarism very cold countries, with good government only possible in temperate regions. We may not be inclined to take such statements very seriously, and indeed they do little to advance the plausibility of Rousseau's general scheme. However, though his judgement on the specifics of environmental factors may strike us as too simplistic and speculative to be convincing, such considerations do make good Rousseau's earlier promise to take 'men as they are' in all their variety. To his credit, throughout Book III he acknowledges the limits of placing abstract political systems into concrete situations. It is something of a strength of his approach that the general framework he advocates is capable of being modified in its details to suit different cultures and conditions. While a full discussion of this topic is beyond the scope of this book, it is perhaps worth noting that the idea of environment, climate and natural resources having a decisive effect on the character of nations and their government is one which is taken seriously in current discussions of international development and political science. Rousseau's precise analysis of the issue may strike us as implausible, but his acknowledgement of it at all may be considered somewhat far-sighted.[16]

Decline and fall (III, 9–11)

Throughout our consideration of Rousseau's political scheme, we have consistently raised the possibility of the state degenerating into the unacceptable forms of despotic government which he is anxious to avoid. A constant worry has been the presence (or lack thereof) of appropriate checks and balances to ward against a state becoming repressive and authoritarian. We have seen that Rousseau at times presents a very optimistic assessment of the matter, in which the sovereign body may be relied upon to guide the community in a reliable and egalitarian manner so long as it is properly constituted. On other occasions, he is much less sanguine about the prospects for success, and introduces the character of the lawgiver to try and ensure that all members of the state exhibit the requisite sense of vision and shared identity. Even then, there have been hints from Rousseau that all but the very best societies will constantly face a pressure to degenerate into less ideal forms of political organization. In the remaining chapters of Book III, Rousseau confronts this issue head-on, and considers how durable his institutional framework is, and under what circumstances it can fail. As we shall see, the sunny tone of his initial presentation of the ideal social order is by no means maintained, and he can seem surprisingly gloomy about the prospects for sustaining the benefits derived as part of the social contract.

Rousseau starts his discussion with a general consideration of what counts as success in government. He points out, consistently enough, that this will vary depending on the nature of the governed people: some will value individual freedom, some tranquillity, some material abundance. The problem with coming up with an uncontroversial measure of social success, according to Rousseau, is that gauges of moral acceptability are notoriously subjective: what one people wants will not be replicated by their neighbours, and so on. Accordingly, he restricts himself to a relatively basic criterion of success: the adequate protection and prosperity of the populace. According to Rousseau, if the people are allowed to participate in the basic institutions of the state and have sufficient material comforts to meet their needs, then the state may be judged a success. The most obvious sign of this is an increase in population: if a nation without widespread immigration increases its numbers then it may be assumed that the government is broadly getting things right.

For the modern reader, this may seem a rather naive measure of success. It is not hard to imagine a very repressive state in which the birth rate is high, perhaps because of government policies to that effect. Indeed, in countries where the ability to provide an adequate living is very insecure, the population may actually rise very quickly as people attempt to offset infant deaths by having more children. Though a rising population *may* indicate a healthy political situation, it does not always do so. For Rousseau's case to be convincing, it would seem to be better to stick to the principles which have thus far acted as the twin criteria for a justly constituted sovereign: the maintenance of equality and civil freedom. If the citizens of the state feel themselves to have, in the most important sense, an equal stake in the life of the community, and furthermore recognize that the unique make-up of its institutions guarantees them a more fulfilling mode of living than they would otherwise have, then the relationship of the sovereign to the government may be said to be successful. Though Rousseau is surely right to claim that such measures are difficult to quantify with any degree of exactitude, they are nevertheless the most important benchmarks against which the success of his project must be judged.

As we have seen, Rousseau is fond of using the analogy of a body to illustrate the health of his social order. The members of the sovereign assembly stand in relation to it as the limbs stand in relation to the body. One guarantee that the sovereign will not harm its members is the argument (of sorts) that a person does not willingly harm their own body. By extending the analogy, Rousseau seems to think that since human bodies invariably decay and die over time, so too does the body politic have a finite existence. Such is human nature that even the best organized states will eventually succumb to corruption and decline. According to Rousseau, this can happen in two ways: the state may contract, or it may dissolve. In the former case, the idea is that once an administration is established, the magistrates will inevitably desire more power, which will lead them voluntarily to shrink the size of the government. To see Rousseau's thought here, suppose that an administration at the 'democratic' end of the spectrum is established. Each magistrate will have a share, possibly quite a small one, in the business of enacting the law. All else being equal, it would be in their interest to increase the slice of government business they control. There is a powerful incentive for each of them to see the total number of magistrates' contract, and for they themselves to remain active within the smaller body. If the sovereign is not alert to this effect, then the remorseless pressure of individual incentives will tend to shrink the size of the government, with a smaller number of individuals gaining ever more influence. The ultimate result of this process is for government to contract to its smallest possible size – an absolute monarchy – which will result in the unhappy relation between the king and the sovereign we have already considered.

According to Rousseau, it is much less likely that the opposite effect will occur – that a small government will gradually increase in size and become more representative – though he does not spend much time arguing for this claim.

The second way in which a state may degenerate is if the government somehow usurps the law-making role of the sovereign and the two bodies become confused. This is actually not so much a separate form of degeneration, but the consequence of the contraction we have just discussed: once a monarch has eliminated all other sources of power within the state, the next step towards domination of the populace is to nullify the competing institution of the sovereign. Should this happen, and the government begins to make the fundamental laws for the community as a whole, then the state constructed along Rousseau's recommended lines has effectively ceased to exist. The laws no longer come from all to apply to all: instead, they emanate from the monarch or the ruling oligarchy, and apply only to those citizens below them in the social hierarchy. The political order has thus reverted to a version of the poorly constituted models rejected by Rousseau at the start of his project. He concludes Chapter 10 with a technical list of terms for these various degenerate societies. The one thing they all have in common is that they may no longer be regarded as genuine instances of a community based on the social contract.

In what follows, the inevitability of this process is spelt out at some length. Since even the great exemplars of Sparta and Rome eventually succumbed to decay, Rousseau argues, what hope can any civilization have of escaping the gradual pull towards corruption? For him, there is no point in attempting to draw up a perfect and everlasting constitutional model: the way of the world is such that even the best polities will fall victim to the ravages of time and the inexorable corruption of human nature. This may strike us as a surprising and troubling conclusion to reach. In what has gone before, the attraction of Rousseau's system has seemed to be the promise of an escape from the fetters of unjust societies. If, as it turns out, such freedom is only every temporary, then Rousseau's scheme appears to present a bleak prognosis for mankind. At best, humans may rise above their capacity to inflict injustice and tyranny on each other only rarely. Even if guided by the exceptional figure of the lawgiver in order to realize their full potential and enter into a society of equality and genuine freedom, sooner or later the edifice will crumble, and the citizens will return to the sorry state from which they emerged. If this is the best that can be hoped for under Rousseau's political system, then we may be inclined to doubt whether it is worth supporting. As we noted earlier, an individual in the state of nature takes a calculated risk in relinquishing their individual freedom to the community: the least they could be expected to demand in return is a guarantee that the resultant state will be of a permanent nature.

In response to this, it could be argued that Rousseau is merely being realistic. If he were to argue that the institutions of his ideal state were by their very nature immortal and incorruptible, then we could be forgiven for finding his whole project implausible. By acknowledging that there is always the possibility that fallible citizens will reject the opportunity of enjoying a better mode of existence, Rousseau is simply reflecting historical and political realities. Moreover, there is no implication on his part that the lifetime of properly constituted states is necessarily particularly short. If a genuinely egalitarian social order could be established which would last, say, for several generations, then that would be an achievement of considerable merit, and an enterprise for which individuals would be rational to take the risk of participating in. Understood thus, Rousseau's vision of an improved social order is not so much pessimistic as simply bounded by a pragmatic awareness of the potential for failure as well as success.

However, if this still seems too gloomy a prognosis to be convincing, then there is a hint in the final paragraph of Chapter 11 that the inevitable decline of societies does not in fact result in a meaningless succession of temporary periods of freedom amidst an otherwise unremitting stretch of despotism. In a suggestive passage, Rousseau remarks that properly constituted societies, even if they eventually dissolve, leave behind a legacy of laws. Where such laws have been determined by a sovereign acting in accordance with the general will, they have considerable legitimacy, and may even command respect once the sovereign itself has disappeared. If, after a period of anarchy or tyranny, a second justly constituted society emerges from the wreckage, it may be able to build on the legacy of its predecessor. In this way, each properly organized society has the potential to improve and augment the achievements of its ancestors. In support of this, Rousseau cites the esteem in which ancient laws are held (we may assume he is referring to the Classical world), and the modified form in which these have been taken on by successor civilizations. Over a very long period of time, punctuated by the rise and fall of various societies, the best legal precedents are strengthened by their repeated adoption. Though Rousseau does not explicitly say so, a reasonable interpretation of this passage would be that humanity is capable of progressing in an absolute sense, even if this involves the constant establishment and rejection of a series of just social arrangements. Just as the individual in the state of nature is able to learn from experience and modify the natural drive of *amour de soi* into a more profound inclination to seek a richer and more fulfilling life, the indication here is that Rousseau believes civilizations too are capable of learning from history, and may retain the capacity to emerge the stronger for having passed through periods where the wisdom of a true egalitarian order has been temporarily forgotten.

In place of strife (III, 12–18)

Whether or not this is the case, Rousseau moves on from a consideration of the failure of societies to a discussion of how the government and sovereign operate when things are going well. He begins by reiterating the essential practical feature of sovereignty, that the assembly of all citizens must meet at regular intervals to establish the laws of the community. Once we have been reminded of this, Rousseau is quick to raise the same objection he made earlier against the practicality of a democratic government: that the logistics of gathering all citizens together in one place will be too much for all but the smallest and most integrated nations. This time, however, he is keen to defend the possibility of such a regular assembly. If such a thing were possible for the Greeks and Romans, he contends, it should be possible in any age. It is only a lack of imagination and shared moral purpose which prevents such regular communal gatherings from taking place. In taking this position, though, Rousseau seems to be directly contradicting himself. If it is too onerous for an assembly of democratic magistrates to meet together regularly, why are things so different where the sovereign is concerned? In fact, it may be even more impractical for the sovereign to come together in a regular fashion, since that body requires the attendance of every adult member of the community, whereas in a democratic government it is only essential that a majority of the population are present.

Clearly, for Rousseau's sovereign assembly to have any practical existence, his society must have a relatively low maximum size.

To make matters more complicated, he also claims that the meetings of the sovereign must be relatively frequent. Under ideal conditions, he recommends, the magistrates may choose to call an assembly at any point in order to deliberate on some important matter arising. In addition, there must be regular meetings which the magistrates have no power to prorogue (presumably partly as a safety mechanism to allow the sovereign to meet even if the government has begun to assert its authority unhelpfully). The precise frequency of the assemblies is a matter for the whole community to decide after taking into account its particular environmental circumstances. However, the clear implication is that in a healthy society the sovereign will convene as often as is practical. As Rousseau acknowledges, the effect of this is to limit the suitable size of the state quite radically. In effect, he has in mind a single town and its environs. Any larger unit would make the frequent gathering of the sovereign unworkable.

Having made these points, Rousseau acknowledges that the upper size limit does pose some questions for his scheme. It seems very restrictive to limit the extent of a nation to single town. As he himself says, small political units are much less able to defend themselves from larger predators (though he does cite the example of the Greek city states which supposedly were able to). There are some other unwelcome consequences of the 'single town' restriction. There may, for instance, be a region in which close cultural connections apply across several separate towns. In such a situation the inhabitants of the region may feel they have a sufficient sense of a shared interest to wish to come together in a single political unit. Such a motivation would be an ideal basis for Rousseau's social system, so it would be strange if the potential union were ruled out purely on the basis of geography. As a result of scenarios such as this, Rousseau does make some concessions. He rejects the idea that sovereignty could be split into several parts in order to cope with a disparate population, but accepts that there may be practical measures which could allow it to cope with several towns within national borders. One would be to devise a form of peripatetic government which could travel around to the various towns in turn. It would perhaps be possible to devise further technical solutions, particularly if we wished to try and implement a Rousseau-esque polity in the modern world where communication is so much easier. However, whatever factors may be capable of being introduced to alleviate the situation, it remains the case that Rousseau feels a small community holds the most promise of sustaining a properly constituted sovereign assembly. The consequence of this, though it may seem rather limiting, is that a country the size of France or Britain has almost no chance of conducting its affairs according to the dictates of the general will. The only nations with a good prospect of organizing themselves according to Rousseau's recommendations are city-states like historical Athens and Sparta, or small entities such as the Swiss cantons.

Aside from the practical considerations involved in convening a sovereign body, there are other reasons, according to Rousseau, for insisting on a small state. It is not enough, he argues, for the citizenry to pay perfunctory attention to the deliberations of the sovereign. For the general will to be reliably ascertained, the members of the sovereign assembly must take their duties seriously and engage properly with the political issues before them. As we have already seen in our discussion of the lawgiver and his mission, for Rousseau the success of the state ultimately derives from the enthusiasm and sense of purpose exhibited by the populace. If this is absent, then the presence of an ideal set of institutions will do nothing to improve the chances of obtaining genuinely enlightened leadership. It is certainly easier to see how a sustained, intimate political involvement might obtain in a smaller community, where cultural and material ties between people will be more readily apparent than in a large and diverse nation. In order to emphasize this point, Rousseau insists that the role of the citizen in the sovereign assembly cannot be delegated to representatives or deputies. Each member of the community must participate in person, and cannot alienate or give away their right (and duty) to involve themselves in the formulation of the state's laws.

It is worth mentioning here that this ban on representation applies to the sovereign body only, not to the government. As we have seen, Rousseau believes that the most successful model of government for most nations is a kind of representative aristocracy in which magistrates are elected to act on behalf of the populace. The reason that this scenario is acceptable is that government is solely charged with the implementation of the law. The sovereign, by contrast, has the more difficult job of establishing the content of the community's basic laws. Should elements of the citizenry delegate their role in the assembly to others, then they are effectively withdrawing from the most important principle of Rousseau's political order: that the laws in every case come from all to apply to all. This is not quite the same thing as opting out of the process altogether, since they are still – in an indirect way – casting their vote on the matters before the sovereign. It is even possible to imagine that a professional delegate or representative of the citizen might be very good at accurately conveying their client's wishes, in which case the reliability of the general will would not be unduly compromised, at least in the short term.

However, Rousseau's worry is over the corrosive long-term effects of a populace excusing themselves from the active job of formulating the laws and leaving it in the hands of a set of intermediaries. Once citizens cease to remain actively engaged in the legislative process, their enthusiasm for the social project will inevitably dim, and they will become increasingly incapable of accurately picking out the good for the entire community. Famously, Rousseau claims that the citizens of England, despite believing themselves to be free as a result of their representative democracy, in fact only exercise their liberty during the relatively rare act of general elections. For the rest of the time, they are subject to the will of their representatives, and are as enslaved as they would be under any other form of tyranny. The example is perhaps not perfectly chosen, since the Parliament of Britain does not have exactly the same role as either Rousseau's sovereign assembly or his government. Nonetheless, the fact that the citizens of England exercised (and continue to exercise) their democratic rights most of the time through a proxy renders their involvement in the political process, for Rousseau, incomplete and unsatisfactory. At best, they are likely while voting to align themselves with a particular party or faction, and due to their habitual state of disengagement will be unable to perceive properly the general will as it pertains to the nation as a whole.

At this point, we may feel inclined to raise the issue of practicality once more. A strength of representative democracy, as opposed to the more direct variant, is that it removes the need for the entire population to be constantly involved with politics. Even in a relatively small polity, the burden of endlessly participating in legislative assemblies may appear ruinously high. In an environment where each individual is also responsible for their own livelihood and that of their families, it might well be thought too much to ask for them to remain focused on the abstract issues affecting the state as a whole on more than an occasional basis. As Rousseau himself acknowledges, the citizens of the Classical world had the advantage of slaves, which enabled them to lead lives of intellectual freedom and enquiry while the necessary business of keeping society going was attended to by others. Amazingly, in a rather worrying lapse, he seems at one point to warm to the institution of slavery as a necessary means of freeing up citizens for the serious business of political engagement. However, he withdraws this speculative thought at the end of Chapter 16, and concludes that, whatever the practical difficulties of maintaining the populace's active engagement with the activities of the sovereign, it is preferable to the situation in which the citizens have delegated away their right to formulate the law, and thereby prevented themselves from the fulfilling kind of civil liberty which only comes from a close and sustained identity with the interests of the community as a whole.

Rousseau concludes Book III with a number of further comments on the relationship between the government and sovereign. The first point he makes concerns the legal establishment of the government. As we know, for a law to be genuinely binding it must not have any particular individual or group as its target. Under this condition, the sovereign can properly legislate to create the institution of government for the good of the entire community, and the administrative system it adopts may be enshrined in law. Once this has been done, the people then have the task of selecting magistrates to take up the various governmental functions (whether by election in the case of a representative aristocracy, or nomination in the case of a monarchy). But in this case the sovereign cannot confirm the chosen individuals in their role, since that would involve singling certain persons out. So the actual business of constituting the government cannot be an act of law. And yet, if the basis of government is not founded on some kind of legitimate process, then its composition will be arbitrary. Rousseau solves this problem by claiming that the sovereign may transform itself into a provisional instance of democratic government solely for the purpose of establishing the magistrates in their posts. Once this has been done, the sovereign reverts to its usual role, and the government, in whatever form it then assumes, takes up its business. Rousseau's second and final consideration is to establish an explicit formal vote at the start of every assembly of the sovereign body concerning two matters: whether the current form of government is still approved by the sovereign assembly, and whether the people wish to leave the government and form a new administration. In this way he hopes to make it obvious that the sovereign is the dominant institution of the two, and that the arrangements for the governmental administration of the state are only ever provisional.

Government and religion (IV, 1–8)

Book IV, the final section of *The Social Contract*, may strike the reader as a rather curious collection of unrelated topics. Whereas Books I and II deal consistently with the legislative basis of a just society, and Book III considers the practical implications of such a system for the business of government, Book IV lumps together three different themes: a further discussion of the nature of the general will, a lengthy treatise on the virtues of the Roman Republic and an important final chapter on the place of religion within civil society. We have already encountered Rousseau's elaboration of the general will, and there is no need to reiterate the points made earlier in any detail. One aspect of Rousseau's treatment of the issue we might remark on here, though, is a series of curious remarks about the survival of the general will even after the dissolution of the state. We have considered a number of ways in which Rousseau thinks the properly constituted society may disintegrate. Under such circumstances, the general will is no longer acted upon, and the community lapses into anarchy or some form of repressive rule. Perhaps surprisingly however, Rousseau still wants to claim that the general will exists, though its dictates are ignored by all. Even if no-one in the society makes any pretence to be acting in the interests of the common good, the general will appears to have some kind of transcendent presence within the society. By using such language, Rousseau seems to be appealing to the notion of the general will in the second of the two senses we identified earlier: not as the motivation existing within each individual to act for the sake of the entire community, but as a kind of independent standard which societies may succeed or fail in conforming to.

Described thus, the general will may appear even more problematic than usual. What kind of thing could it be, if divorced from the actual practice of individual desires and decisions? One answer would be that it must be a kind of divine benchmark against which the concrete wills of individuals could be judged. Another might be that using the term in such a way is something of a fudge on Rousseau's part: a vague use of language which, under examination, might collapse back into the slightly less nebulous notion we have been using more generally. However, referring back to the points made above about the cumulative effect of successive just-ordered societies, we might advance the following tentative thesis. The general will, used in its most common sense, is the name given to the motivation each individual has to act in the interests of the community as a whole. We may also use the term to describe the decision actually made by the sovereign assembly which reflects the best average of all these general wills across the whole community. If the sovereign body is acting correctly and the social institutions are functioning as they ought, then these two senses of the general will are very close together: the latter is simply a refinement of the former. However, as we have seen, it is possible for even the best societies to dissolve over time. If this happens, with any luck they will leave behind them a legacy of law which may be picked up by successor nations. Over a very long period of time, the practices which continually survive this process, and which are repeatedly found to be beneficial and useful, garner a certain authority of their own. Once this body of generally accepted laws and practices reaches a certain level of maturity, it may become appropriate to describe its most fundamental maxims as a kind of 'universal' general will. In much the same way that the deliberations of the sovereign refine the will of all into the general will of the community, the process of advancement and decay which all states are subject to refines the various general wills of past communities into a set of standards which all nations may aspire to.

Such an interpretation is very speculative, and has been constructed here on scant foundations. However, it does capture something of the flavour of the general will as a standard or benchmark against which healthy societies must attempt to measure up. Whether or not it accurately reflects Rousseau's thought here, it seems clear that he believes the general will has some kind of existence or significance in isolation from the actual willing of members of a sovereign body, and that even when the conditions of the social contract have irretrievably broken down, there still remains some sense in talking about the dormant 'general will' of the state.

In Chapters 4–7, Rousseau leaves his exposition of the general will behind and spends some time explaining the virtues and vices of ancient Rome. His purpose here seems to be to lend weight to the arguments previously advanced on the rise and fall of civilizations. In among a number of topics, he considers the best form of elections, the potential rise of dictatorship, and various sorts of tribunals established by the Romans to help arbitrate between different moral and legal visions of society. To the modern reader, the discussion may well seem of strictly historical interest only. Strangely, Rousseau does not draw many explicit parallels between the Roman model and his own social framework. It may be that he thought the links between the two would be obvious, or simply that the insertion of such a treatise would lend a certain gravitas to the argument of *The Social Contract*. In any case, it demonstrates once again the indebtedness Rousseau felt towards the example of the Classical world in formulating his own political vision.

Of most interest in Book IV, however, is the final chapter on civil religion. In this self-contained passage, Rousseau expounds his views on the extent to which the state may have jurisdiction over its citizens' religious beliefs. His conclusion is that, in the interests of the common good, the state does have a role in regulating the beliefs of its constituents, but that it is of a particular and restricted sort. Rousseau's stipulations here have seemed to his critics to present another example of his totalitarian tendencies. To see how his thought develops, and whether this criticism is justified, we will have to follow his chain of reasoning throughout the chapter, which progresses from a theory of the origin of religion, through a comparison of three basic types, to a final verdict on what kinds of beliefs ought to be tolerated by the justly constituted state.

Rousseau starts by making some bold claims about the genesis of religions. In the earliest days of civilizations, he claims, each tribe or nation had their own god. To be a member of a certain nation was more or less the same thing as believing in a certain god. As a result of this, there were no religious wars in the sense that Europe was familiar with, with different nations battling over the interpretation of a common theology. Instead, it was understood that each nation had its own deity, and every member of the polity owed allegiance to that deity in the same way that they owed allegiance to the tribe. Now, as we know, Rousseau places great store by citizens' sense of loyalty to and identification with the state, and believes that if this is not present then the community cannot prosper. When the dictates of religion and the nation are coexistent, there is no conflict between the two. However, if the demands of religion separate from the demands of the state, then the social fabric risks being damaged. According to Rousseau, the rise of the monotheistic religions, Christianity especially, exemplifies this process. The unique feature of religions like Christianity is that they demand allegiance to a spiritual realm which is clearly different from the citizen's temporal jurisdiction. The result is a conflict of allegiance on the part of every citizen between the state and the Church. In the case of the Catholic Church, Rousseau claims, the separation is particularly acute, since, for the French at least, the seat of spiritual authority is located in an entirely different country.

Once he has given this historical sketch, Rousseau then goes on to isolate three different kinds of religious belief. The first he calls the religion of man, which seems to be an expression of the simplest kind of reverence for the Supreme Being and the dictates of morality. As we noted earlier, Rousseau is by no means in opposition to the idea of a natural divine law, and appears to view the religion of man as a kind of pure consciousness of this supernatural order. In its unadorned state, the religion of man is less concerned with doctrine or ritual, and more with fostering a sense of brotherhood on earth and an anticipation of the bliss awaiting in the afterlife. This simple devotional sentiment is succeeded by the religion of the citizen, which is the pre-Christian state we have just encountered. Here, the individual awareness of the sanctity of the moral order is replaced by an elaborate construction of rituals, dogma and legally sanctioned forms of worship. Finally, this system is replaced by the religion of the priest. This is the name Rousseau gives to a doctrine, like Christianity, which has isolated itself from the interests and identity of the state and which demands allegiance to a higher set of institutions.

For Rousseau, all three kinds of religious belief are inimical to the smooth running of a justly constituted state. The religion of the priest distracts citizens from the proper object of their loyalty and diverts their energies elsewhere. Under such circumstances, the people can no longer be relied upon to identify their interests with the state, as required by the lawgiver, and will at best have their loyalty split two ways. The religion of the citizen, while preserving a single object of devotion among the citizenry, is little better, since it promotes manifest falsehoods and empty dogmas. Finally, the religion of man is in some ways the worst of all, as it advocates an unworldly conception of life and diverts the citizens away from the concrete demands of their social duty. Rousseau complains that there is nothing worse for the social spirit than having the attention of the populace detached from the world and diverted to considerations of the hereafter. In practical terms, therefore, every kind of religious belief has poor consequences for Rousseau's social objectives.

After such an analysis, one might expect Rousseau to advocate atheism for the citizens of his ideal state. However, Rousseau believes that atheists are the worst kind of people of all, since they (in his account) can have no certain ground for personal morality. As a result, atheists would be the most unreliable and least moral types of citizens of all, and must not be tolerated in any justly conceived political order. In the light of this, Rousseau's response to the problem of religious belief is therefore rather surprising. A 'civil creed' will be drawn up which contains a small number of core beliefs. These are: that there exists a supreme being which foresees and provides, that there is an afterlife in which the just are rewarded and the unjust punished, that the social contract and the laws emanating from its institutions are sacred and inviolable, and that intolerance for any other religious belief not in contradiction with these maxims is forbidden. The penalty for failing to adhere to these maxims is either deportation from the state or, in the most extreme case, execution.

Stated thus, Rousseau's views on religion seem at once cynical and repressive. In a manner reminiscent of the lawgiver's aping of divine authority, we might be wary of Rousseau's apparent entirely pragmatic dogma of the sanctity of the social contract and its laws. This seems to be a purely artificial requirement of the creed, simply inserted in order to maintain social cohesion and loyalty to the state. Certainly, Rousseau does not argue for any genuine theological basis for of his political model, and it seems to be inserted into the creed as a matter of simple expediency. Moreover, the draconian punishments meted out to any who refuse to publicly profess such a creed appear repressive in the extreme. We are apt to think of religion as a matter of personal conscience, and to respect the freedom of every individual to reach their own conclusion on such matters as the existence of God and an afterlife. By making these subjects matters for the state, Rousseau certainly seems to be breaking his promise to leave citizens of the ideal state as free as they were before entering into it. The only positive part of the scheme appears to be the requirement of tolerance for other religions, so long as the beliefs in question do not contradict the basic maxims of the civil creed. Since Rousseau's dogmas are very general, it would certainly be possible for some religions to coexist with such a creed. However, many religious people would reject the notion that the social contract, or any man-made political arrangement, has the same level of sanctity as the belief in God or an afterlife. Anyone who publicly professed such a thing would face deportation from Rousseau's state. Accordingly, even Rousseau's attempt to foster a degree of tolerance in his social order seems to hold the promise of oppression.

Rousseau has identified a critical issue in his treatment of civil religion: the potential conflict of interest arising from mixed allegiances. His response, consistently enough, is to insist that identification with the state comes first. The motivation for this can be given a positive gloss, in that Rousseau genuinely believes that the potential for human happiness and fulfilment is only possible through close identification with the state and the general will of all its members. However, it is surely hard for the modern reader to support the methods Rousseau advocates for settling the issue. In laying down a strict prohibition on atheism, as well as promoting doctrines which seem to have no genuine root in an honest appreciation of the divine, Rousseau's view on civil religion as expressed in *The Social Contract* is one of the least attractive aspects of his entire theory. Thankfully, his system as a whole does not seem to demand its adoption. It would appear perfectly plausible to remain committed to a social model constructed along Rousseau's lines, including the insistence that citizens possess a close identification with the state and a strong commitment to the general will, and yet allow space for personal religious conviction (or lack thereof).[17]

SUMMARY

Having now covered the entire text of *The Social Contract*, it is perhaps worth drawing some threads together. As we have discussed, Rousseau's political philosophy – his conception of the institutions and laws best fitted to enabling people to live in a state of equality and freedom – is founded on prior notions of psychology and a vision of human nature. Without some understanding of these ideas, his scheme loses much of its rationale. Of primary importance here is Rousseau's consistent worry about the potential of individuals to prosper in a situation where their individual wills are placed together in an environment of mutual and involuntary dependence. Of equal importance is his belief that, if a way could be found to remove those shackles of dependence, then the positive natural inclinations which we all share may be harnessed in a more fruitful direction. The shape of the society created by the social contract can only make sense if viewed through this prism.

We have repeatedly raised the question, which seems particularly natural from a classically liberal perspective, of the lack of 'checks and balances' in Rousseau's account. What is there to stop the sovereign abusing its considerable power? How can the members of the community have a clear knowledge of the general will? What prevents them from ignoring its dictates? Though it is clear that Rousseau does vary somewhat in his responses on this point, the fundamental answer to this question lies in the essential goodness of human beings, and their (sometimes latent) capacity to work together in the interests of themselves and those around them. If this inherent ability can be channelled, perhaps through the agency of an inspirational leader, into a social framework, then the system will be self-regulating. However, this success is only ever provisional. There always remains the possibility that even the best societies will degenerate and ultimately dissolve. In such a case, the best that can be hoped for is that they will leave a legacy of just law which may be picked up by others.

As we have seen in our discussion of government, in many ways Rousseau advocates a system very similar to representative democracy, and as such some of the accusations of totalitarianism which have been levelled at him are therefore wide of the mark. Elsewhere however, particularly in his discussions of the death penalty, the inviolability of the social contract and the place of civil religion, his instincts do give a liberal critic plenty to worry about. As such, the moral acceptability of his scheme remains an open question. As noted before, the fact that his polity has never been implemented, at least properly, makes it hard to gauge to what extent it would have a genuinely repressive character in the real world. Of course, each reader of *The Social Contract* must judge for themselves what the consequences of Rousseau's political order would be, and whether they sympathize with the underlying structure he presents. However, even if doubts remain over the ultimate acceptability of Rousseau's ideas, or whether his scheme truly delivers on the promise to provide genuine equality and freedom while guaranteeing security, it should be evident that the ambitious task he sets himself throws up a number of important issues for political philosophy which remain of primary importance. The uniqueness of *The Social Contract*, which makes it difficult to place within the wider stream of political thought, lies in its radical diagnosis and original cure of one of the deepest problems of the individual within society. As a sympathetic and influential commentator writes:

> The significance of *The Social Contract* lies in its attempt to articulate the legitimate basis of political authority in the rule of the people over themselves, and in its account of the manner in which the people authorize their own terms and conditions for association through the acts of the general will. There is continuous controversy over the interpretation of many points, especially over whether Rousseau, while professing to be concerned with the freedom and dignity of the individual, does not in fact make him a slave of the whole community. But in its absolute affirmation of the equal rights of all citizens, of their standing as members one with another of the sovereign body, it remains a work of radical import.[18]

Certainly *The Social Contract* has proved extremely influential in both the theory and practice of politics, and in philosophy and psychology more generally. The following chapter considers a few of the ways in which this has taken place.

STUDY QUESTIONS

1. What is the role of the government in Rousseau's political system? How does this relate to the role of the sovereign? Would such a relationship function effectively?
2. What types of government are possible in Rousseau's state, and which have the most chance of success? Do you agree with Rousseau's diagnosis of the strengths and weaknesses of the various systems?
3. What are the causes of social decline, according to Rousseau? Are they convincing?
4. What are the reasons for Rousseau's suspicion of religion? Does his response adequately resolve the issue?
5. Taking *The Social Contract* as a whole, do you feel that Rousseau succeeds in his mission of presenting a society where both freedom and equality are guaranteed?

CHAPTER 4

RECEPTION AND INFLUENCE

In one of Patrick O'Brian's novels set during the Napoleonic Wars, the acerbic ship's surgeon Stephen Maturin leaves his companion in no doubt as to his opinion of Rousseau's influence on Europe:

> I have no patience with Emmanuel Kant. Ever since I found him take such notice of that thief Rousseau, I have had no patience with him at all – for a philosopher to countenance that false ranting dog of a Swiss raparee shows either a criminal levity or a no less criminal gullibility.[1]

Such sentiments would have been shared by many Britons of the nineteenth century, for whom Rousseau was an exemplar of dangerous continental extremism. Even during his own lifetime, Rousseau had a peculiar ability to inspire both adulation and downright loathing. There have been very few commentators then or since who have taken a lukewarm position on his character and thought: he tends to strike his readers either as a muddle-headed charlatan or a secular prophet of signal importance and vision. What is beyond question is that, for good or ill, *The Social Contract* and other writings by Rousseau have profoundly influenced political theory and practice. In this chapter, we will trace some of the historical responses to the text as well as some more modern treatments.

POLITICAL RESPONSES

As we have seen in our discussion of his life and times, Rousseau was quite capable of alienating even his closest supporters with his erratic behaviour and accusations of conspiracy. He went from being a confidant of many of the chief figures of the French Enlightenment – Diderot and d'Alembert among them – to a figure on the fringes of the *philosophes*. Yet even in the darkest days of his mental disturbance and paranoia, he always maintained a devoted following among some members of the establishment. His novel *Julie, or the New Héloïse* was wildly popular. Many readers were also excited by the controversial sentiments expressed in *Émile*, which even more than *The Social Contract* exercised the conservative religious authorities. These enthusiasts for Rousseau's literary output were initially more numerous than advocates of his political writing. As a result of this, even during his enforced peregrinations around Europe, Rousseau still retained powerful friends and protectors, one of whom arranged for him to travel to England with the philosopher David Hume when his persecution was at its height. As noted earlier, the two fell out and Rousseau returned to France, with the affair only adding to the controversy which perpetually surrounded him.[2] Hume, one of the great philosophers of the age, seemed not to warm to Rousseau's political philosophy at all, claiming that the belief that *The Social Contract* was of more interest than *Julie* was as absurd as the belief that Milton's *Paradise Regained* was superior to *Paradise Lost*.[3]

After Rousseau's death in 1778, his literary notoriety blossomed into something of a cult of personality. His house at Ermenonville was turned into a shrine, and visitors came to pay their respects from all over France.[4] The ideas of *The Social Contract* were not principally behind this enthusiasm. Rousseau's political thought received relatively little interest immediately after his death, and his accomplishments in other fields remained the main driver of his fame. All of this was to change, however, with the coming of the French Revolution. In the decade leading up to 1789, France suffered increasingly from poor financial management and a series of ruinously expensive wars. Rousseau's prediction that the kings of Europe were doing all they could to create the conditions for violent revolution was therefore somewhat prescient. The most obvious result of the maladministration of Louis XVI was a marked deterioration in the conditions of those at the lower economic end of the social spectrum. Widespread famine, malnutrition and unemployment created an atmosphere of resentment among the bulk of the populace against the excess and luxury of the monarchy. Political agitation and unrest grew steadily throughout 1789, culminating in the iconic moment of the Revolution: the storming of the hated Bastille prison in Paris.

In the turbulent period thereafter, the monarchy was overthrown, and France was transformed into a revolutionary republic.

For the leaders of the revolutionaries, Rousseau was an important inspiration. His ideas of communal ownership and resistance to the tyranny of unelected monarchs were very much in tune with the views of the progressive factions in France fighting for change. Robespierre, one of the chief architects of the Revolution, claimed to have been greatly inspired by Rousseau, and explicitly drew on his political philosophy as the intellectual basis for the establishment of a new political order in France. In 1794, Rousseau's remains were transferred from Ermenonville to Paris in order to be placed in the Panthéon, the resting place of the heroes of a new, egalitarian France. Copies of *The Social Contract* were carried by members of the entourage surrounding his coffin. The transformation of Rousseau the author of novels and composer of operas to Rousseau the political philosopher had taken place. The Revolution needed an intellectual basis for its radical policies, and he seemed to many to be the ideal candidate. When the time came for the revolutionaries to devise principles on which to base their new society, the language they chose was strikingly similar to passages from *The Social Contract*. Clause VI, for example, of the revolutionaries' *Declaration of the Rights of Man and of Citizens* reads:

> The law is an expression of the will of the community. All citizens have a right to concur, either personally, or by their representatives, in its formation. It should be the same to all, whether it protects or punishes [. . .].[5]

This statement clearly derives from the idea of a general will, and the notion that the law comes from all and applies to all. Indeed, Robespierre was to claim that the dictates of his Committee of Public Safety, a powerful instrument of control during the period when the revolution degenerated into the 'reign of terror', were the very embodiment of the general will. Clearly, Rousseau's ideas permeated deep into the consciousness of the Revolution.

As a result of his alleged inspiration for a movement which quickly became a byword for political repression, Rousseau has received considerable criticism. The English conservative opponent of the Revolution Edmund Burke called him an 'insane Socrates' for his role in inspiring the excesses and brutality of the French Republic.[6]

However, it is certainly open to question how justified the revolutionaries were in aligning their project with Rousseau's. Though there is much in *The Social Contract* which would have appealed to them, notably Rousseau's arguments against an unelected sovereign monarch and for the legitimacy of resisting it, it is far less clear that the political order they imposed in its place was at all a genuine implementation of his ideas. As we have seen, Rousseau envisaged his social order operating at a fairly small level: a city-state or canton. There is very little in *The Social Contract* to suggest that he thought it practical to try and govern a state the size of France according to his institutional framework. One obvious reason for this is the impracticality of convening a truly inclusive sovereign body over such large distances and involving so many people. Indeed, the power assumed by partial bodies such as the Committee of Public Safety is precisely the kind of thing Rousseau wished to ward against with his lengthy and oft-repeated claim that the laws passed by the sovereign must come from all to apply to all. Given the many differences between Rousseau's stated policies and those enacted during the Revolution and its aftermath, it must be doubtful how many of Robespierre's counterparts had actually read *The Social Contract* with any insight, no matter how much they may have held Rousseau up as their model.

So while Rousseau may have provided the spark of inspiration which drove opposition to France's authoritarian administration, the differences between his views and those of the revolutionaries are stark. Although his name is often spoken in the same breath as those of the revolutionaries, it would be inaccurate to claim that their aims and methods were in any genuine sense derived from the precepts of *The Social Contract*. Nonetheless, the inspiration it provided for the many progressive movements across Europe chafing against an apparently overbearing political system should not be underestimated. We have seen that Rousseau's rhetorical powers are extremely strong: he has a distinct gift for coining a memorable phrase or aphorism. Although this on occasion can make it difficult to see precisely what his pronouncements amount to, the force of his language is undeniable. It was capable of inflaming the sentiments of Robespierre and his counterparts, and it has retained its power to inspire and motivate political revolutionaries ever since. Many of Rousseau's key themes have been adopted by other thinkers keen on establishing a following for their ideas. Consider the famous conclusion of another influential political treatise: 'Let the ruling classes tremble at a Communistic revolution: the proletarians have nothing to lose but their chains.'[7] This is part of the rallying cry at the end of the *Communist Manifesto*, another small book which has had a tremendous effect on political ideas and practice, and for which Rousseau is also held responsible by many.

Certainly, there are key notions in common between Marx's philosophy and Rousseau's. Both make much of the unhappy state of humanity as it exists within poorly constituted societies, and the need for such unequal social orders to be replaced by one with a shared vision and sense of the communal good. Marx and Rousseau both had an abhorrence of class-based slavery and the arbitrary rule of monarchs over the masses, and both advocated an alternative political scheme where the interests of the community as a whole would be enacted. Moreover, there are psychological ideas Marx obtained from Rousseau via the tradition of German Idealist philosophy which were instrumental in his conception of the human condition and the resultant optimal shape of social institutions. In particular, we can recognize Rousseau's influence on the Marxist concept of alienation. Perhaps most importantly, the cornerstones of Rousseau's project: equality and civil liberty (freedom realized through the institutions of the state) were to become vital aspects of Marxism as well.

Of course, the proper interpretation of Marx's vast body of thought is a particularly vexed issue, and the task of identifying the genesis of certain ideas is always liable to be controversial. Nonetheless, if we extend our ambit slightly to consider the broader political movement of socialism rather than the more ideologically charged Marxism, it seems clear that Rousseau's ideas were of instrumental importance. As we have seen, Rousseau had a decidedly ambivalent attitude to private property, and generally believed that it should be placed in trust to the state as a whole. He was uniformly pessimistic about the chances that individuals operating in accordance with their own drives and inclinations would resist the slide into malign *amourpropre*. As a result of this human frailty, Rousseau felt that the only solution was the imposition of a powerful state in which each member would be forced to accord with the dictates of the general will of the community. As we have already discussed, this vision of social organization relies on a version of 'positive freedom', an idea which is closely associated with the socialist project.

For those critical of the totalitarian nature of some socialist states (such as Soviet Russia), there are uncomfortable notions in Rousseau, such as the deceptive activities of the lawgiver and the rights of the state over life and death, which seem to prefigure the worst excesses of those regimes. Certainly, it is possible to criticize Rousseau for the somewhat cavalier manner in which worries of this nature can appear to be treated. However, we have also drawn attention to the mechanisms which Rousseau believed would safeguard his state against tyranny and the imposition of repressive government. There is certainly little similarity in conception between the small communities of individuals freely contracting themselves to work together in accordance with their general will, and the vast despotisms established during the twentieth century in the name of socialism and Marxism. Once again, the extent to which Rousseau may be held responsible for the unattractive features of actual states is a matter of fierce controversy.

ENLIGHTENMENT, ROMANTICISM AND AFTER

Aside from Rousseau's contribution to concrete political change, the ideas of *The Social Contract* have been similarly influential in the wider sphere of ideas. We have already drawn some attention to his participation in the French Enlightenment. Like all such intellectual movements, it is difficult to state with any precision or cohesion what the exact aims and beliefs of the architects of the Enlightenment were, but several central themes do assume prominence. One is the lack of deference paid to traditional forms of authority, such as religion and monarchy, and a desire to subject even basic beliefs to rational scrutiny. As such, Rousseau's political thought is certainly in tune with the iconoclastic spirit of the age. His thorough reformation of the very basis of the political order, working from first principles through to the conclusion, is a project firmly in the spirit of the Enlightenment. His rejection of politics of tradition and precedent, best exemplified by Grotius and Filmer, mark him out as a theorist of his time. Perhaps most of all, his insistence on the essential moral dignity of mankind and the need for an equitable political system to enable this natural capacity to flourish sits squarely in the mainstream of the Enlightenment project. In previous ages, the key desideratum of any political system would have been adherence to the natural law as laid down by God. By placing 'men as they are' at the heart of his system, Rousseau is reflecting the confident spirit of his age, in which man and his rational faculties provide the foundation for all inquiry into the best kind of social organization.

However, much of what Rousseau advocates is also significantly out of sympathy with the general direction of the Enlightenment. As we have previously discussed, he was consistently sceptical of the benefits of technological and scientific progress. While his contemporaries marvelled at the great strides being made by the application of reason, Rousseau was more concerned with the corruption of humanity's inherent goodness and simplicity. Throughout *The Social Contract* he is concerned to try and replicate, in some senses at least, the conditions of a pre-civilized state where competition for and exploitation of social status are not the principal activities of those in the state. As we saw in our examination of the general will, Rousseau thinks that simple-minded folk are the most able to conduct themselves in such a way that guarantees the prosperity of the community. It is the sophisticated, educated classes, for Rousseau, who have been responsible for leading society into its ruinous state. Rather than celebrating the achievements of his contemporaries, the inspiration for his ideal state comes from the provincial Swiss cantons and the historical example of the Classical world. Such provincialism, arguable lapsing into sentimentalism on occasion, is very much out of the sympathy with the tenor of his intellectual peers.

As a result of this profoundly ambivalent attitude towards the Enlightenment movement, Rousseau is also identified with its successor, Romanticism, which is an even more difficult period to define. Whereas an essential feature of the Enlightenment was a prevailing belief in the power of reason, the corresponding element of Romanticism is perhaps more of a privileged role for the emotions and a rejection of the rationalization of the natural world. The Romantics were wary of the efficacy of a permanently cool and detached manner of engagement with the world, and preferred to characterize the ideal life as one where the passions were given adequate licence to operate. The best way of establishing and understanding the proper environment for humanity, according to such a view, was not to operate consistently on a rational level, but to revel in the full struggle and contradiction of a world seen through the prism of the emotions. The spirit of the age is best captured by the great literary works of Wordsworth, Byron, Goethe and Schiller. All these figures knew of Rousseau, and several referred to him with approval. Of all his works, the candid and tortured *Confessions* was most in tune with the movement, but there are certainly aspects of *The Social Contract* which prefigure important trends in Romanticism. Rousseau's continual appreciation of the natural goodness of people and the usefulness of all their inherent drives and inclinations is the most important feature in this regard.

So Rousseau's influence in the history of ideas is somewhat complex. Perhaps more so than any of his peers, his vision is difficult to place neatly into any intellectual category. Like other great thinkers, he occupies a position all of his own, and to align him too closely with any intellectual tradition would risk misrepresenting the uniqueness and vigour of his work. In the field of academic philosophy, he has certainly been taken up as an inspiration by a diverse range of figures. We have already touched briefly on Marx, but among those others in debt to Rousseau is one of the giants of German philosophy, Immanuel Kant, who seems to have drawn great inspiration from Rousseau when formulating his own political philosophy, as well as his extremely influential moral theory. According to Kant, when considering the rectitude or otherwise of a given course of action, it is the intention behind the action that is more important than the consequences. The essential moral quality for an individual to cultivate is a good will. Kant's rules for determining right and wrong actions in the light of this are quite complicated, but an important aspect of them is this: an individual should act only according to that maxim by which they can also will that the action would become a universal law. In other words, the only right actions are those that apply universally in the sense that everyone has a reason to assent to them. Already in these words we can perceive something of an echo of Rousseau's conception of the general will. And elsewhere, Kant is even more obviously in debt to Rousseau:

> A rational being belongs to the Kingdom of Ends as a member when, although he makes its universal laws, he is also subject to these laws. He belongs to it as its head, when as a maker of laws he is himself subject to the will of no other.[8]

Here the inspiration from Rousseau's idea that the only legitimate kind of law comes from all and applies to all is clear.

In more recent times, Rousseau has continued to provide inspiration for philosophers and political theorists. The most influential of these has been John Rawls, whose *Theory of Justice* has been credited with reviving interest in political philosophy since its publication in the 1970s. As his starting point, Rawls takes up a very similar question to Rousseau: what mechanism can we use to determine a universally binding set of fair principles of justice and governance, given that all of us have different individual desires, abilities and demands? The solution he adopts shares some important features of Rousseau's system. First, Rawls adopts the contractual model: the promise of a fair society is made possible if the participants in some sense agree to be bound by the laws. He also makes use of a procedure analogous to the state of nature in Rousseau's account, which he calls the 'original position'. This is a hypothetical state of affairs prior to the establishment of the social order, the most important feature of which is that each individual is subject to a veil of ignorance concerning their role and status in the future society. When charged with making the contract to join together as a political unity, therefore, they have no interest in making the conditions unequal, since they do not know what position they will occupy. If the social principles are such as to guarantee a high degree of equality, as least as far as certain fundamental rights and goods are concerned, then individuals will have a good reason to accept them. The similarity between Rawl's hypothetical basis for the state and Rousseau's actual decision procedure is striking, and he acknowledges his debt to the idea of the social contract:

> What I have attempted to do [in *A Theory of Justice*] is to generalise and carry to a higher level of abstraction the traditional theory of the social contract as represented by Locke, Rousseau and Kant.[9]

Rousseau, then, occupies a position of more than historical importance. His ideas continue to help shape contemporary responses to problems of political right and equality. Though there are elements of *The Social Contract* which today receive relatively little attention (such as Rousseau's analysis of the Roman Republic), it is remarkable the extent to which the text continues to inspire debate and discussion. The effects of *The Social Contract* are both profound and various, and if one wishes to develop an understanding of contemporary political thought and practice, of moral philosophy, or even of human nature and psychology, it remains of the utmost value.

NOTES

1. CONTEXT

[1] Grotius's most influential book is *The Laws of War and Peace*. It is upon this extensive treatise that his reputation as the father of international law is based. His discussion of a populace giving up their rights to a ruler, which Rousseau makes much of, is in Book III, Chapter 7 and onwards ('Of the Right over Prisoners'). A discussion of Rousseau's relationship to Grotius (and Hobbes) can be found in 'Rousseau and the Friends of Despotism' in *Ethics*, Vol. 74, No. 1.

[2] Rousseau, *The Confessions*, p. 20.

[3] Rousseau, *The Confessions*, p. 327.

[4] Rousseau, *Reveries of the Solitary Walker*, p. 27.

2. OVERVIEW OF THEMES

[1] Rousseau is, at the least, ambivalent about the potential of women to enjoy the same level of moral and intellectual development as men. In *Émile*, the female counterpart of the eponymous protagonist, Sophie, has a firmly supportive and subordinate function. In what follows, I shall generally assume that Rousseau's social and political theory applies to both men and women, but it should be remembered that he would have principally had men in mind when discussing potential citizens. For a further discussion of this, see Wokler, *Rousseau*, pp. 100–102, and Dent, *A Rousseau Dictionary*, pp. 248–249.

[2] Rousseau, *The Confessions*, p. 377. At this stage, the work in question was a more ambitious project called *Political Institutions*. This larger study was never completed, and *The Social Contract* is a shorter compilation of some of the central themes.

[3] Locke, *Two Treatises of Government*, §4 (p. 116). See §§4–15 for a fuller account of this, taking into account some objections. The contemporary political philosopher John Rawls, in his influential *A Theory of Justice*, also uses a variant of the idea of a pre-social state in his concept of the 'original position'. See the final chapter of this book for a brief discussion of this.

[4] Rousseau, *Discourse on the Origin of Inequality*, p. 161.

[5] Rousseau does in fact remark on this difficulty in the *Discourse on the Origin of Inequality*, and states that his claims should not be taken as

historical fact, but as hypothetical conjectures. But it seems clear from the detailed survey which follows that he does at least want his claims to be taken seriously, and sees them as an accurate account of human psychology.

6 Rousseau, *Discourse on the Origin of Inequality*, p. 188.

7 Rousseau, *Discourse on the Origin of Inequality*, p. 184.

8 A critical appraisal of Rousseau's account of the state of nature can be found in J. C. Hall, *Rousseau: An Introduction to his Political Philosophy*, pp. 28–73. See also Christopher Bertram, *Rousseau and the Social Contract*, pp. 33–36.

9 Rousseau, *Discourse on the Origin of Inequality*, p. 182 (n. 2).

10 Rousseau, *Discourse on the Origin of Inequality*, p. 182 (n. 2).

11 This account of *amour-propre* is taken from Dent's *Rousseau: An Introduction to his Psychological, Social and Political Theory*, especially pp. 70–72, where there is a much fuller account of the notion and its role in Rousseau's wider psychology. In what follows, I shall generally refer to *amour-propre* in its malign or 'inflamed' sense in order to contrast it with the wholesome *amour de soi*. The reader should be aware, however, that not every reference to *amour-propre* in Rousseau's *oeuvre* carries a necessarily negative connotation. See also Dent and O'Hagan, 'Rousseau on *Amour-Propre*', *Proceedings of the Aristotelian Society, Supplementary Volumes*, Vol. 72, pp. 57–73.

12 The contemporary mathematician and historian Joseph Gautier believed this, but Rousseau specifically rejected his suggestion. See Wokler, *Rousseau*, p. 23.

3. READING THE TEXT

1 Rousseau, *Discourse on the Origin of Inequality*, p. 203.

2 Filmer's basic argument can be gleaned from the titles of the three chapters of his influential book Patriarchia: '1. That the first Kings were the fathers of families', '2. It is unnatural for the people to govern, or choose governors'and '3. Positive laws do not infringe the natural and fatherly power of kings'. He takes scriptural authority as the basis for establishing the just principles of governance, and is a strong critic of representative government and democracy.

3 See Hobbes, *Leviathan*, Chapter XVIII (p. 122). We shall briefly touch on Hobbes's account later on.

4 For Aristotle's presentation of the idea that some are fitted to be slaves while others are fitted to be rulers, see Aristotle, *Politics*, Book I Chapter v (1254a17–1255a3).

5 Hobbes, *Leviathan*, Chapter XVIII (pp. 121–122). Some minor alterations to the format of the text (removal of italics, etc.) to aid legibility.

6 This was given as his inaugural lecture. It has been reprinted several times, most recently in the collection *Liberty*, pp. 166–217.

7 For a discussion of Locke's views on property, see his *Two Treatises of Government*, especially Chapter 5 of the second treatise.

8 Locke is often held to have been the originator of the concept of the separation of government into the legislative and executive arms. His

discussion of the matter can be found in the *Two Treatises of Government*, §§143–148 (pp. 188–190).

[9] We'll see this as we consider more of the text. For an illustration of the range of expectation, see *SC*, I, 7 (especially paragraph 5), and then *SC*, II, 6 (especially the final paragraph).

[10] I shall follow Rousseau's usage and use the male pronoun, though there seems nothing in the text which would automatically debar the lawgiver from being a woman.

[11] For a fuller discussion of the techniques used by the lawgiver, see Christopher Kelly, '"To Persuade without Convincing": The Language of Rousseau's Legislator', in the *American Journal of Political Science*, Vol. 31, No. 2 (321–335).

[12] Rousseau, *Émile* (Book I), pp. 39–40.

[13] For a wide-ranging discussion of Rousseau's conception of the proper status of the individual and community, see Katrin Froese, 'Beyond Liberalism: The Moral Community of Rousseau's Social Contract', *Canadian Journal of Political Science*, Vol. 34, No. 3 (579–600).

[14] Shortly after *The Social Contract*, Rousseau was to begin work on a legal framework for Corsica, then fighting a war of independence against the Genoese. The work was never completed, but a fragment survives as the *Project for a Constitution for Corsica*.

[15] For a fuller discussion of this point, see Frank Marini, 'Popular Sovereignty but Representative Government: The Other Rousseau', *Midwest Journal of Political Science*, Vol. 11, No. 4 (451–470).

[16] For an influential popular account of this thesis, see Jared Diamond, *Guns, Germs and Steel: The Fates of Human Societies*.

[17] This is a very brief sketch of Rousseau's views here. A much fuller discussion of the place of religion in the civil state is found in Bertram, *Rousseau and The Social Contract*, pp. 177–189.

[18] Nicholas Dent, *A Rousseau Dictionary*, p. 225.

4. RECEPTION AND INFLUENCE

[1] Patrick O'Brian, *Treason's Harbour*, p. 7.

[2] A recent entertaining history of this is David Edmonds and John Eidinow, *Rousseau's Dog: Two Great Thinkers At War In The Age of Enlightenment*.

[3] The remark comes from Hume's correspondence. The reference is taken from Dent, *A Rousseau Dictionary*, p. 25.

[4] For an account of the extent of this, see Gordon McNeil, 'Rousseau and the French Revolution' in the *Journal of the History of Ideas*, Vol. 6, No. 2 (197–212).

[5] This extract is taken from Dent, *Rousseau*, p. 216.

[6] See Wokler, *Rousseau*, p. 77.

[7] Karl Marx and Friedrich Engels, *The Communist Manifesto*, p. 258.

[8] Immanuel Kant, *Groundwork to the Metaphysics of Morals*, quoted in Dent, *Rousseau*, p. 219.

[9] Rawls, *A Theory of Justice*, p. xviii.

FURTHER READING

1. WORKS BY ROUSSEAU

The text of *The Social Contract* in French, along with all Rousseau's other published works, may be found in the *Oeuvres Complètes*, ed. by B. Gagnebin and M. Raymond (Paris: Éditions Gallimard). Volume III, published in 1964, contains the full text of *The Social Contract*, the *Discourse on the Sciences and the Arts* and the *Discourse on the Origin of Inequality*. Volume I (1959) contains *The Confessions* and the *Reveries of the Solitary Walker*, and Volume IV (1969) contains *Émile*.

A separate edition of *The Social Contract* in French has been published with an English introduction by C. Vaughan (Manchester: Manchester University Press, 1955).

There are a number of English translations of *The Social Contract*. The one used throughout this guide has been by Maurice Cranston (Harmondsworth: Penguin, 1968). There is also an edition of *The Social Contract and Discourses* translated by G. D. H. Cole, augmented by J. H. Brumfitt, J. C. Hall and P. D. Jimack (London: Dent Everyman, 1993). A more recent translation is found in *The Social Contract and Other Later Political Writings*, ed. by Victor Gourevitch (Cambridge: Cambridge University Press, 1997).

Extracts from the *Discourse on the Sciences and Arts* and the *Discourse on the Origin of Inequality* were taken from *The Social Contract and Discourses* translated by G. D. H. Cole, augmented by J. H. Brumfitt, J. C. Hall and P. D. Jimack (London: Dent Everyman, 1993). They are also available from *The Discourses and Other Early Political Writings*, ed. by Victor Gourevitch (Cambridge: Cambridge University Press, 1997).

Extracts from *The Confessions* were taken from the translation by J. M. Cohen (Harmondsworth: Penguin, 1953).

Extracts from *Émile* were taken from the translation by Allan Bloom (New York: Basic Books, 1979).

The Extract from the *Reveries of the Solitary Walker* was taken from the translation by P. France (Harmondsworth: Penguin, 1979).

There is also an edition of Rousseau's complete works in English, currently in progress. At the time of writing, six volumes have been released, which cover all of the works referred to in this guide, including *The Social Contract*. See *The Collected Writings of Rousseau*, ed. by R. D. Masters and C. Kelly (London: University Press of New England, various dates).

2. BOOKS ON ROUSSEAU

There are numerous commentaries on Rousseau's work and life in general, and *The Social Contract* in particular. Some of the most useful are:

Bertram, Christopher, *Rousseau and the Social Contract* (London: Routledge, 2004)

Dent, Nicholas, *Rousseau: An Introduction to his Psychological, Social and Political Theory* (Oxford: Basil Blackwell, 1988)

Dent, Nicholas, *A Rousseau Dictionary* (Oxford: Blackwell, 1992)

Dent, Nicholas, *Rousseau* (Abingdon: Routledge, 2005)

Edmonds, David and Eidinow, John, *Rousseau's Dog: Two Great Thinkers at War in the Age of Enlightenment* (London: Faber & Faber, 2006)

Gildin, Hilail, *Rousseau's Social Contract: The Design of the Argument* (Chicago: University of Chicago Press, 1983)

Hall, J. C., *Rousseau: An Introduction to his Political Philosophy* (London: Macmillan, 1973)

Miller, James, *Rousseau: Dreamer of Democracy* (New Haven, CT: Yale University Press, 1984)

O'Hagan, Timothy, *Rousseau* (London: Routledge, 1999)

Shklar, Judith, *Men and Citizens: A Study of Rousseau's Social Theory* (Cambridge: Cambridge University Press, 1985)

Wokler, Robert, *Rousseau* (Oxford: Oxford University Press, 1995)

3. ARTICLES ON ROUSSEAU CITED IN THE TEXT

Dent, Nicholas and O'Hagan, Timothy, 'Rousseau on Amour-Propre', *Proceedings of the Aristotelian Society, Supplementary Volumes*, Vol. 72 (57–73)

Froese, Katrin, 'Beyond Liberalism: The Moral Community of Rousseau's Social Contract', *Canadian Journal of Political Science,* Vol. 34, No. 3 (579–600)
Kelly, Christopher, '"To Persuade without Convincing": The Language of Rousseau's Legislator', *The American Journal of Political Science*, Vol. 31, No. 2 (321–335)
Marini, Frank, 'Popular Sovereignty but Representative Government: The Other Rousseau', *Midwest Journal of Political Science*, Vol. 11, No. 4 (451–470)
McNeil, Gordon, 'Rousseau and the French Revolution', *Journal of the History of Ideas*, Vol. 6, No. 2 (197–212)

4. OTHER MATERIAL REFERRED TO IN THE TEXT

Aristotle, *Politics*, trans. by T. A. Sinclair, rev. by T. Saunders (Harmondsworth: Penguin, 1987)
Berlin, Isaiah, *Liberty*, ed. by Hardy, Henry (Oxford: Oxford University Press, 2002)
Diamond, Jared, *Guns, Germs and Steel: The Fates of Human Societies* (W. W. Norton, 1999)
Filmer, Robert, *Patriarchia and Other Political Writings*, ed. by Johann P. Sommerville (Cambridge University Press, 1991)
Hobbes, Thomas, *Leviathan*, ed. by Richard Tuck (Cambridge: Cambridge University Press, 1996)
Locke, John, *Two Treatises of Government* (London: Dent, 1993)
Marx, Karl and Engels, Friedrich, *The Communist Manifesto*, ed. by Gareth Stedman Jones (Harmondsworth: Penguin, 2002)
O'Brian, Patrick, *Treason's Harbour* (London: HarperCollins, 1997)
Rawls, John, *A Theory of Justice* (Cambridge, MA: Harvard University Press, 1999)

INDEX